Nursing the Wounds

Nursing the Wounds

TWO NURSES' EXTRAORDINARY STORY OF *faith* AND *overcoming* SEXUAL ABUSE

by *Dawn Compton* and *Amanda Schrader*

XULON PRESS

Xulon Press
2301 Lucien Way #415
Maitland, FL 32751
407.339.4217
www.xulonpress.com

Unless otherwise indicated, Scripture quotations taken from the King James Version (KJV) – public domain.

Scripture quotations taken from the New Century Version (NCV). Copyright © 2005 by Thomas Nelson, Inc. Used by permission. All rights reserved.

Scripture quotations taken from the Holy Bible, New International Version (NIV). Copyright © 1973, 1978, 1984, 2011 by Biblica, Inc.™. Used by permission. All rights reserved.

Scripture quotations taken from the New King James Version (NKJV). Copyright © 1982 by Thomas Nelson, Inc. Used by permission. All rights reserved.

Printed in the United States of America.
Edited by Xulon Press.

ISBN-13: 9781545629918

This book is for the millions who feel voiceless, powerless, and defeated. For those who are silenced, for those who are coerced into being quiet, we speak for you.

We see you. We see your hurting hearts. We see you struggling through your day-to-day lives. We see you acting out of a place of pain.

And so does God.

We know there is hope. We've been there, and we've come out on the other side.

We have always said that if this whole experience—the journey, the book, the message, our social media pages—if it touches only one, it will have all been worth it.

There are so many more than one, and we see you.

TABLE OF CONTENTS

PREFACE

*D*awn and Amanda are two nurses with an extraordinary story. Seventeen years prior to working together, they crossed paths at a backyard Bible club in rural Mississippi in the summer of 1999.

Amanda was a nine-year-old girl who had been raised in an atheist home. Dawn was a teenage volunteer with her church—a church that chose to bring God into the community.

Years later, they would find each other again in their chosen career in a different town, with a similar story as survivors of sexual abuse and a similar desire to one day tell the world. God had the plan that would bring it all together.

God has an amazing way of connecting dots. His plans for our lives are so complex, so beyond our imagination, if only we would open ourselves up to be vulnerable to His will.

ACKNOWLEDGMENTS

First and foremost, thank You, my Lord Jesus Christ, for turning this pain into purpose. The most beautiful story of my life is the one You are authoring. Thank You for going to such great lengths to capture my heart. Thank You also for giving me my friend Amanda, for saving our souls with such amazing grace, and for weaving us into each other's story in such a beautiful way.

Thank you, Corey, for always pushing me out of my comfort zone. Although this particular journey has been difficult for you to understand, I appreciate your support more than you know.

Thank you to our two daughters for always inspiring me to be better. I love you both so much, and I pray that this legacy shines a light for generations to come.

Thank you, Brother Jamie and Brandi, for making me feel acceptance for our platform and validation that there is a place for my story in ministry. Thank you also to our church family that has been so wonderfully supportive.

Thank you, Amanda, for who you are!

To every person who has lent a listening ear to me over the years, thank you. There are so many of you who have shown me love, and in that, you have shown me the true character of God.

—*Dawn*

*M*y God, You are my strength and the best part of my testimony.

A special thanks to Ryan, my loving husband, for the endless prayers. You've never given up on me even when I gave up on myself.

For my precious boys, I pray that you know strength and persevere in all things, and that you always turn to God. This legacy I leave for you. Mommy will always be an advocate for you two until the end of her days.

For my mom, this was never a burden for you to carry. I love you more than you know.

For Dawn, thank you for being a light in a very dark time for me. I am beyond grateful for your friendship.

To each and every person who has helped me along this journey, the open ears and hearts and endless prayers have not gone unnoticed or unappreciated.

For my siblings—the truth!

—*Amanda*

DAWN—INTRODUCTION

At the time that I write this, I am thirty-six years old. For reasons unbeknownst to me, at my last birthday, I had an epiphany of sorts: thirty-six felt as if it would be a year of completion. As thirty-seven quickly approaches, I know now this was God's way of inserting a bit of foreshadowing into my story.

Writing, to me, is a very healing art form. It is a way to displace emotions into a tangible form—a record of heartaches and joys. I have always sought refuge in my writing, but in recent years, I had abandoned it due to responsibilities that took priority over my own personal development.

I have always wanted to tell the world my story in hopes that it would help someone else, but I haven't really had clear direction on how it would all take place until this year. I have always felt that God would provide the opportunity, since He placed the dream in my heart, and He certainly did not disappoint.

Birthdays and holidays tend to be a difficult time for me, as they are for a lot of people for one reason or another. For me, memories of these events tend to leave me feeling empty and a bit depressed. I'm not inviting you to my pity party; I'm just being honest.

You see, my first twelve years were spent in confusion and torment, as you will read; my second twelve years were introspective, as I was left to interpret the first twelve years; and this third twelve were spent in healing. As you read my story, it will be broken into these twelve-year sections to explain my experiences during those times. If truth be known, I have been writing my story for years, as you will see from the excerpts I'll include along the way.

CHAPTER ONE

DAWN: THE FIRST TWELVE

Train up a child in the way he should go: and when he is old, he will not depart from it.
Proverbs 22:6 KJV

*L*ife is a temporary heaven or hell, depending on what you make of it. Mine has been a journey, sometimes a maze, of learning, growing, heartache, restlessness, independence, observation, trusting, and mind maturing that has at times tripped me while I was unaware. At times, coincidence seemed to be such an ever-present theme, but then I adopted the thought that I did not believe in coincidence; I believed in God. I will say this: there were many times that life seemed unfair. Sometimes it was a true struggle, and yet as I look back on my life now, I have no regrets. Were the events of my childhood unfortunate? Yes, but they are a part of my story, and I can't change my story. I would not be who I am today.

To understand where you're going, you have to understand where you've come from. In the same sense, I believe to understand who you are, you have to understand where you came from. To understand me, and to get a glimpse of what my childhood was like, you must first look at my parents.

I was born from a highly unlikely marriage.

My father was born in 1915 on a rural farm in Mississippi. He had an exceptionally interesting life. His father, by all accounts the stern patriarch, served as a judge on the local circuit. His mother died in childbirth when he was young; however, his father soon remarried, and the family continued to grow to become a family of eleven.

My father and his siblings worked on the family farm, as many children did in that time, and never finished school. He left home around twenty years of age after signing on with the United States Army. Later, he worked as a guard at the Panama Canal. He got out of the army only to again sign up when World War II began, and when he did, he eventually worked his way up to become a staff sergeant. He responded to a call for volunteers, and the lure of a "dangerous mission," which would later identify or destroy who he was as a man. The mission turned out to be the Merrill's Marauders—the original Army Rangers, of which my father was an original member. This group of brave men gained national recognition for their heroic bravery and were awarded a Bronze Star and a Presidential Unit Citation.

After the war, as best as I can gather, my father traveled a good bit. He moved to Chicago, and after thirty-two years, he eventually retired from a steel factory there. During his time in Chicago, he also married and had a daughter. Years after they divorced, my father married my mother.

When I was younger, my parents explained to me that they were "pen pals." I later understood this to mean that they met through a service that paired American men with foreign women. Some people would call this a mail-order bride service. It was essentially a rudimentary version of modern online dating services. After my dad began corresponding with my mom, he flew to the Philippines to meet her, got married to her while he was there, returned Stateside with his new wife, then retired and moved back to Mississippi.

My mother was born the youngest of four sisters in the Philippines in 1947. Her mother passed away when my mother was two years old. In the formative years that followed, my mother was without a mother. Her father did not remarry for ten years, but when he did, the family continued to grow until there were ten daughters and two sons. Although the family was tightly knit, my mother's stepmother treated the first four sisters unfairly, and my mother resented her for years.

Life was difficult on the rural island. Money was tight between the two adults and their growing brood of twelve children. My mother dreamed of a day when she would be able to leave that little island to earn a living. As soon as she could work, she quit school and held a string of positions as a nanny for foreign families.

When my parents moved to Mississippi, I can imagine it was a difficult transition for not only my father (having been away for many years), but also for my mother, who had no friends or family close by and very little grasp of the English language or culture. Nevertheless, they settled into a small three-bedroom brick home in the country, right next door to one of my father's brothers and his wife. There were many other sisters and brothers who lived locally. The sisters taught my mother how to cook the Southern home-cooked meals that my father preferred, and my mother tried her best to emulate the qualities of a stereotypical Southern housewife.

My father chose to live very frugally, and having a wife who was from a third world country suited him, as she considered herself lucky to have fresh water to be able to wash clothing, sheets, and towels by hand to hang out on the clothesline. I literally had no idea how to use a washer and dryer until college, when I was left to figure it out for myself.

Three years after my parents married, I was born. My memories of childhood up until I was old enough to go to school consist of those that include my family. My dad would not allow my mother to work, and he was retired, so they were both at home all of the time. We never went on vacations. We rarely ate fast food, except on the rare occasions when my father would agree to get hamburgers when we went to town to the grocery store. I think we went to the local zoo one time when I was a child. That is pretty much the extent of any childhood outings that I remember with my parents. The rest of our time together consisted of visiting my father's elderly friends and family in the area, which usually resulted in my boredom.

Because of how sheltered my father chose to live, my mother explained to me on several occasions how I, unbeknownst to her, skipped kindergarten. When it was time for me to start first grade, I had to have a place-ment test to make sure that I was ready for school. I was. Luckily, my parents, most likely from their own experiences, always instilled the importance of education in me. I remember my mother's delight in how I would make up stories from my interpretation of pictures in books as soon as I was able to talk. By the time I started school, I knew how to read, and my father had taught me basic addition and subtraction.

I also remember driving by the local university campus on many occasions, usually after a trip to the grocery store, and my parents explaining to me that one day I would go to college there. I was always in awe of the beautiful campus—the rose garden, the duck pond, the large buildings—and the thought that one day I would be there. Years later that childhood dream would come true, and not only would I claim this school as my alma mater, but I would teach there as well.

My aunt and uncle lived next door to us, and I remember walking to their house almost daily from the time I learned to walk. My parents had several fruit trees they had planted in the "holler" (Southern slang for a valley) between our homes, and in the summer, I would usually stop to pick a handful of ripe plums off the ground. Then I would stop at the fence post at the corner of my aunt and uncle's property and smell the fragrant honeysuckle. I'd walk past the willow tree in the front yard with both adoration and scorn. Though it was absolutely beautiful with its wispy branches, I had to pick my own switch from it on several occasions for punishment. I'd stroll onto the breezy carport, fling open the screen door, and announce my arrival.

Screen doors in the South are a way to let the breeze in without letting critters such as cats, dogs, and mosquitoes in. This particular screen door had a tight spring; once you learned that, you made sure to clear the threshold quickly, lest the aluminum door bottom catch your Achilles. I actually remember my uncle using this same door to assist in pulling some of my loose teeth as a young child. Someone—probably my aunt—would hold the door open as he tied a string around the tooth, being sure there wasn't much slack in the string between the door and my tooth. The anticipation of the door closing was the worst. You never knew whether the door was going to take you with it or whether you would be left a bloody, painful, crying mess. Surely this kind of thing happens only in the South.

In addition to pulling my loose teeth, my uncle would take me for rides on his tractor and drive me to church on Sundays. It was a small country church, but I remember being introduced to the love of Jesus Christ there at a very young age. My parents never attended. My father had grown up Baptist, and my mother Catholic, and although they felt that church was important, my mother, for one, did not have a driver's license to go to Mass on her own, and two, because of her strong ties to her Catholic faith, did not want to attend a Baptist church. My father had no interest in attending the Catholic church.

My aunt was always very kind to me. She would help me with my penmanship and give me stationery on special occasions. She also taught me to crochet. One of my favorite treasures that we would make was crocheted cross bookmarks. One day my aunt and uncle gave me my very own Bible as a gift. I used one of the purple crocheted crosses that I had made with my aunt as a bookmark. I was so proud to have a Bible of my own, complete with a loving inscription written on the inside from my aunt and uncle.

There are fundamental questions in a little girl's heart that are answered by the adults in her life at a young age. *Do you love me? Am I worthy?* These questions are answered not only by verbal responses, but nonverbal ones as well. Time is a gift that you can't get back; that's why *right now* is considered a present. So many times my aunt and uncle answered these questions for me with the amount of time that they spent with me, as well as the way they doted on me. It was not uncommon for me to spend whole days with them, especially during the summer months when school was out.

Let me preface the rest of my story by telling you to understand as you read this, there were things that did not make sense to me as I was growing up. As you grow up, everyday things do not seem out of the ordinary. You are just learning how the world works, and you're acclimated to your own version of "normal." You trust everyone, because adults are to be trusted, not questioned. They're supposed to be there as your guardians, your mentors, your liaisons between your present and your adulthood.

There were things that didn't set right in my spirit, but truth had to be revealed to me in God's perfect timing. There were things that happened, as you will read, that were absolutely wrong, but there were also things that happened that were absolutely right. Our lives are a puzzle, where we sometimes get pieces that don't fit together right then, but later we find out exactly why those seemingly insignificant pieces were there all along.

There were times, too, that I felt so much fear in and around my own home, but I didn't quite understand why. I remember one time in particular when I was about ten years of age. I was home alone, but outside in the yard because I didn't want to be inside the house alone. It started raining, and our house was locked. I knew where the spare key was, but I really didn't want to go inside the house alone, so instead, I sought shelter underneath the aluminum slide of my swing set, which faced our house. I remember an ominous feeling that the house itself was looking back at me, watching me, and if not the house, *something* was looking back at me. I remember staring back at our dark house and feeling a negative energy, as if the house were alive, and a fight-or-flight fear completely held me captive until my parents arrived home shortly after.

Understand as you read that I grew up in a house that was not God-fearing, but yet I had reverence for God. My aunt and uncle saw to it that I was in church on Sundays, and I am so grateful for that. What I learned in Sunday school was permanently etched in my heart and laid the foundation of faith for some very troublesome times ahead.

Lastly, understand that when people refer to their "normal" childhood, I have no idea what this means. I never could conceive of this; I never knew what a normal childhood consisted of, and if I ever considered my childhood as normal, it was a lie. I might have held on to any morsel of normalcy I had, but what I had was certainly not normal.

———◆◆◆———

When I started school, I excelled at it. I was comfortable at it. I could challenge myself with it, and I did. It was an escape. I was the first person out of my grade to test for the gifted learning program at my school, and for a long while, there were only the gifted teacher and I. I have a lot of fond memories of making origami and working independently through the puzzles she tasked me with. School quickly became something I could dive headfirst into without worrying about negative consequences.

As far as my environment at school, I did not feel this same comfort. I was honestly so wrapped up in my own head most of the time that I now know I was suffering from a good bit of social anxiety, even as a first-grader. I remember episodes of urinating on myself that first year of school, which should have been a red flag, but it wasn't. I also remember vomiting on several different occasions on the school bus from becoming nauseated by the noise and motion sickness, so much that my bus driver finally started sitting me on the tiny little metal ledge right between her and her window—something that would never happen in this day and time in our state of safety-consciousness (this was the eighties).

It was around this time that I also realized I wasn't totally white, which was ironic because White was my last name at the time. Other kids noticed too, and they made sure to point it out to me. To add to my confusion, my family was racist, and I began to pick up on that. I never could understand how my father or his family could be racist when I wasn't even white. From that point forward, I had the mentality that no one could ever truly understand me.

My mother was also subjected to the same mentality, although it was subdued, but I still could discern it. It was as if she were "lesser." Sure, they made an effort to throw me a nugget of normalcy when they were around her, but she was different, and that was pretty palpable. My father's family was very skeptical of my mother when they first married, an attitude that would transcend a generation and also set the precedent for future struggles.

I always felt like I had to protect my mom. As a kid, I remember being so scared that people weren't going to accept her because they didn't understand her. It was easy to be embarrassed of her. Her English was never perfect, and she would periodically yell out to me in public by calling out—very loudly, mind you—in a deep, throaty voice, "Hoy!" (the Filipino equivalent for "hey"). It's funny to picture now (as if it weren't obvious that I was her half-Filipino child), but I would sometimes pretend as if I didn't know who she was and continue to walk on.

I mentioned before that I never knew any of my grandparents. My maternal grandfather was the only living grandparent I had when I was born, but he lived in the Philippines, and I never had a chance to meet him before he died. I remember the day we found out he had passed away. There was a string of phone calls that ended with my father hanging up on the caller abruptly each time, then confusion, then my mother crying. All of a sudden, I remember the heavy receiver of our big, red rotary phone being handed to me. It was one of my mother's friends who lived locally, and she was explaining to me that my mother was sad, and I had to be a big girl. Years later I found out that my family in the Philippines had tried to call my mother collect, but my father wouldn't accept the calls. They finally reached my mother's friend, whom I spoke with, and she was the one to deliver the bad news of my grandfather's demise to my mother. My mother never forgave my father for that.

I am my parents' only child together. I know I have at least one half sister (this statement will make more sense later on). My first cousins are all about twenty-five years older than I am, so I was always closer in age to my second and third cousins. I had one cousin—we'll call her Tia—who was more like a sister to me than a cousin, and we shared much of our childhood together.

Tia's grandmother, another aunt of mine, would usually have dinner at her house for everyone on Sunday afternoons. Her house was always full of people—family, friends, and neighbors. This aunt also took care of yet another aunt, my Aunt Belle.

Aunt Belle was diagnosed with schizophrenia in her early twenties. Soon after, she was committed to the state mental health facility, where she lived for several years. The treatments my aunt had to endure during this time were unheard of. No one ever talked about it. It was taboo, but it fascinated me. One time there were whispers of electroshock therapy; then another time, mention of a partial lobotomy. I still do not know the extent of all she had to endure; it was a different era of medicine, and she was a ward of the state, something else I overheard.

My Aunt Belle was terribly misunderstood. If I learned any lessons from my father's family, it was that if people cannot understand you, they make their own assumptions and think what they want to anyway. If you are not understood, you are not a part of them. My Aunt Belle was an outsider in our family, and I identified with her in that.

Some Sunday afternoons, Tia and I would listen to Aunt Belle "talk." She had a chair in the living room next to the piano, which Tia and I pretended to play, but our true interest was in what Belle might say when she didn't think that anyone was listening. Aunt Belle would start talking, not to us, but to whoever it was in her mind that was talking to her. I learned so much about her just from listening to her—whom she liked, whom she couldn't stand, random things about the people she talked to—but there was also an air of mystery surrounding the things she said. Why was she talking to these people? What in the world had caused her to have this condition?

One particular afternoon, Aunt Belle headed off to her room for an afternoon nap. Another cousin of ours crawled into her room. Tia and I were never that brave, but we watched in amazement. She crawled right up under Aunt Belle's bed. Tia and I crouched at the cracked doorway, holding our breath, trying not to snicker. As she lay in her bed, Aunt Belle began to talk again. Our cousin looked at us, still peeking in from the doorway, from underneath the bed with a proud grin across her face. Aunt Belle continued to talk for what seemed like hours, and then suddenly, midsentence, she yelled to that cousin underneath her bed, by her name, to "get out from under my bed!" The cousin rolled out from under the bed and scurried out of the room, mortified. After that incident, we didn't listen in too much. I realized that my aunt was more lucid than she seemed, but dealing with a lot of demons from her past.

There were other things that I experienced during those years too—unspeakable things that happened behind closed doors, right next door to my home, that no one cared to acknowledge. I was sexually abused for the first eleven years of my life. It was my normal. I knew no different. Most people who lived in that town would eventually find out about my uncle, as you will read, but I have never told my story—my testimony—like this.

My aunt and uncle's living room was set up in such a way that where my uncle sat in his chair could not be viewed by where my aunt sat in her chair. I know—it is bizarre, and looking back now, I feel certain that these things were on purpose, and that she turned a blind eye on the abuse. If you can picture an L-shaped room where the bottom leg (wall) is the focal point and where all of the furniture faces, the small part where that bottom leg juts forward has an inside corner section that is not visible from the opposite vertical leg (wall). My uncle's chair sat on that inside corner facing the television, and my aunt's chair was along that opposite, longer wall, faced in the same direction but positioned near a window.

My uncle's chair was a place of pure torture. It was a place where he would pull me in and make me his plaything. I was no longer the little girl whose loose teeth he pulled with the screen door that so quickly recoiled. I was no longer the little girl that he made sure was in Sunday school. I was no longer his niece that he looked after as if he were a grandparent. I was fair game for him. It wasn't just him having his way with how he wanted to touch me; he would also force my hands on him. I will never forget the disgusting feel of his semi-erect penis in my hands as a child, with his hands tight over mine.

During the abuse, he would coax me into affirming that I liked what was happening. He would force me to believe that this was *normal*, and this was my *duty*. It was a *privilege* to sit with him in his chair. He was *choosing* me. I was *lucky*.

I remember that during one episode, I had brought one of my dolls to their house. He began to touch my doll inappropriately and talked about how "grown" my doll was. I remember getting the impression at that time that as I "grew," he would take more delight in me, and it made me feel awfully confused about myself. If the worth

17

of a woman was measured by her chest size, then I was obviously not worth anything yet, but here was this man who could not keep his hands off me.

On so many of those occasions, I distinctly remember my aunt in the kitchen with her back turned toward the living room. I was focused on her so many times during these episodes. She always had her long gray hair secured in a loose bun with a net and bobby pins. She wore skirts that hit her at midcalf or modest dresses that were right below the knee. She often wore an apron, especially if she had been making something with flour. She always seemed to take an extraordinary amount of time washing the dishes or just standing at the sink looking out the kitchen window, always so careful not to turn around.

Among other things that I remember are the constants: his denim overalls—a staple of my uncle's wardrobe—and how the green faux leather on the armrests had begun to rip, most likely from the frequent weight of children on them. I remember that in the summertime, the rough breaks in the fabric felt as though they were cutting the underside of my thighs. I also remember afternoons that I was forced to lie down and take a nap in the bed with both my aunt and uncle.

To add to the horror, sometimes Tia or some of the other local children were with me while the abuse was happening. At times, he would involve multiple children in his forced abuse. His armchair was a torture chamber, and I was his daily victim.

Please understand that I never had a parent, or any adult for that matter, tell me that what my uncle was doing to me was wrong. If you are reading this and you have small children, you need to start having this conversation *now*. I started explaining right touch versus wrong touch to my children when they were toddlers in words that they could understand. There is no shame in this. It is your duty as a parent.

I did not know any different, as this was a daily occurrence for me, but there did come a time when I started to realize that something wasn't quite right. Then suddenly everything changed. One day, when I was about eight years of age, my best friend told me that my uncle had touched her and she thought it was wrong, and she wanted me to know that the way he was touching me was wrong, too. This friend actually came from a very religious family, and looking back now, I see she approached me like an adult about it. She was direct, she was truthful, and she was wise beyond her years. All of a sudden, I was shamed into facing what was happening. I remember exactly where we were when she began to have this conversation with me and was emboldened to tell my parents as well. We had gone across the county to visit my dad's sister but arrived to an empty home. This was the era before cell phones, when life was much simpler, much slower. I remember we just waited. We must have sat on the porch for an hour or more, just sitting in the old wooden rockers overlooking their large pond. I can't remember how she brought it up, but she did. It seems like there were a few questions, and then it was over. No more questions. This was the first and only time in my childhood that anyone stood up for me and stood up for what was right. I'm not even sure if she ever told her own parents. From this day forward, I had an awareness deep down—a *knowing*—that I did not have before, but I was still powerless to do anything about it. It wasn't long afterward that my best friend moved with her family out of state.

One day a series of events was set into motion that would change my life forever. When I was around nine years of age, a new family moved into the next house down the road from us. They had three children, who ranged in age from about four to eight. The oldest was a girl, a redhead with a fiery personality who was the "boss" of her younger brother and sister. I don't remember much else about them. I don't think I was around them a whole lot; however, the "grandparents" of the neighborhood, my aunt and uncle, took them in just as they did everyone else, and my uncle's predatory nature eventually took over.

The next memories that I have involving Tia and that family down the road are from when I was eleven. I remember being in a state of total fear, holding our family's cordless telephone tightly to my ear, talking to Tia in my front yard. I remember the anticipation of hearing the pop of a gunshot at any time. I remember it was dusk, just dark enough to see blue lights flashing. A sheriff's deputy was at my uncle's house. It's all a blur now, and I'm not quite sure how the series of events happened. The little redheaded girl from next door told her mother what had been going on. My uncle had been molesting the kids next door for several months. Tia, too, told her grandmother, who in turn told Tia's father, and her father wanted to kill my uncle for what he had been doing to his daughter. My uncle was arrested that night.

His case was highly publicized. The story was broadcast on the local news almost daily. At that time, we only picked up the local news channels, but they all seemed to cover the unfolding drama more regularly than what I was comfortable seeing. Every time there was a court date, the whole viewing area was informed of the details. I stopped watching television; it was a mortifying experience as a preteen to see your darkest secret high-lighted on the nightly news. I lost friends because, of course, parents didn't want their kids to come home with me. I was very reclusive. I was humiliated. I lied to people at school who asked if I was related to him. I was depressed.

I became socially withdrawn and depressed. I asked my parents about putting me in counseling, but my father would not agree. I begged because I knew I needed help. I knew what I was going through was not normal; I should not have been having suicidal thoughts at twelve. I was afraid to die, but I couldn't fathom living another day bearing the burden that I carried. I vividly remember contemplating suicide. It was a hot summer, as usual, and I was lying on our couch staring up at the ceiling, crying—literally crying—out to God to help me. I was raised in southern Mississippi. I knew how to use a gun. I had my mind made up that this was the way that I would end things, but then something began to stir within me. I cried out to God to save me from myself. I cried out to God because I did not understand. The whole situation felt so unjust; I never thought I would be able to live through it.

My parents did not address the abuse, nor did the rest of the family. I remember being made to sit across the table from this uncle on a Sunday afternoon while he prayed over our food. He could not make eye contact with me. I was so disgusted. To add insult to injury, my father's family shamed my questions, my unforgiveness, my desire for justice. At this point, I had no friends, no family (sure, I had people I was related to, but no one but Tia really understood what I had been through), and no church family for support. I felt completely alone, left to interpret my situation as best as I knew how as a child.

Not once during this time was I ever approached by any adult—no teacher, counselor, law enforcement officer— literally no one. I had never felt so alone. I remember one day my mother was speaking to one of her friends on the phone. The friend told her that one of the teachers at my school had called me a "loner." I didn't know what that word meant at all, but I remember this moment changed something within me. I had lost trust not only in my family, but now in every single adult in my life. I remember the distinct thought of, *Who gossips about a kid? How terrible is this world that an adult would have nothing better to do than to talk negatively about a child?*

I recall one time in a junior high math class that a classmate asked me if I was related to (he then proceeded to say my uncle's name). Ironically, I lived just off a road that was named after my uncle. At some point during my childhood, this practice had been implemented within the county to honor the eldest person who lived on each road. Since I shared his last name, lived right next door, and lived in a very small town, it was correctly assumed that we must be related. This kid rode past my house on an almost daily basis for baseball practice. He knew exactly where I lived, exactly where my uncle lived. Fear and shame struck my heart, and I recoiled. He asked me if the very man who had caused me so much pain and anger was family to me. *Family* —the very word hurt for the longest whenever it was implied. I panicked. My mind quickly went into fight-or-flight mode, and I looked for a way out. I lied when I replied no.

I know it probably wasn't, but my uncle's court case seemed like the longest drawn-out case ever. It was all over the news. When I went to school, I felt as if everyone knew. I was paranoid. I wanted to die. I withdrew from people, and I put on a mask toward the people that I had to have contact with. I lived in a minefield of "what if" situations that I navigated with extraordinary pre-cautionary measures to avoid any perceived danger, especially if those situations might cause me potential embarrassment or shame. I think a lot of preteens begin to develop this sense of awareness around the same time that I did; however, mine was fueled completely by my experience of abuse and the publicity that my uncle's case received.

Whereas most kids started to wear name brands so they would stand out, I wanted them to blend in. I didn't want any more attention called to me than what I perceived was being spoken about me in secret. Most kids did whatever was necessary to be popular; I did whatever was necessary to get by to move forward. Graduating from high school and moving on was my mission. I made grandiose plans in my mind to move away from the small town of big hurts and envisioned what my life would be like. Little did I know that God would have His hand on my life after I cried out to Him in prayer to save me from myself.

The summer after my sixth-grade year, right after my uncle's arrest, I was able to get away for a little while. It was the greatest escape for a little girl from a little town who was living in the midst of a huge nightmare. I had no idea what adventures awaited me by boarding the first flight of my life. I experienced a certain relief and juxtaposition to see my small world from the sky above. I felt as if I were leaving a chaotic life that was in shambles for something better. *Isn't that what God intended?* I thought.

My mother and I spent the entire summer in the Philippines. That summer was the most magical summer I've ever experienced. The backdrop certainly added to the effect; the country is one of the most beautiful places on earth. I met my family for the first time. I know that sounds so funny, but previously we knew each other only through pictures and letters.

I found something within my Filipino family that I was missing in my American family—a sense of true loyalty. It was not the kind of loyalty to cover up wrongdoing at the expense of generations, but true dedication to each other to help and defend each other however they could. I saw my mother through different eyes as she relaxed around what was familiar to her. She knew how to navigate through the idiosyncrasies of her culture, and I was completely dependent on her to guide me.

We toured landmarks, temples, beaches, and parks. Everything was a dream that I could not have ever imagined. We stayed with family in different regions of the country. On one particular visit, one of my aunts gave me the gift of a pig for my upcoming birthday. It was a peculiar gift maybe, but my aunt had very little and this animal was a lot for her to give away. I affectionately named my new pet Wilbur.

Traveling in and around the Philippines was most interesting. Inland, we used buses, jeepneys, or side cars, which were small carts attached to bicycles, dirt bikes, or motorcycles. To the outlying islands, we flew, bussed over long bridges, or took a boat. On one particular occasion, we loaded Wilbur into a large wooden crate and boarded a ferry for an overnight trip. We were to sleep on the open deck, which was lined with rows of cots, and when we woke up, we would be on the island where my mother was born and raised.

A teenager on the boat with a group of kids gravitated toward me and seemed to try particularly hard to befriend me. All of the kids were curious about me because I looked different from them. This was the same experience I had back home, except this seemed more positive on the surface. The short-haired teen was masculine and had a huge smile. I found out this person was going to the same barrio where we would be staying. I was glad to be in the company of people who genuinely seemed interested in me. The next day when we arrived, as we were preparing to exit the boat, the teen grabbed my backside in the most inappropriate way, and suddenly a million fears rushed over me in the most uncomfortable of ways. *What is it about me that makes people think they can just grab me?* I thought. I thought I had escaped from those feelings, but it seemed as if they had followed me to the other side of the globe.

I later told my mother, who told my uncles, and those uncles, unbeknownst to me, confronted the teen that I had thought to be a boy. The teen was actually a girl, however, and they told the girl to stay away from me. They defended my honor. On one hand, I felt extremely loved because my uncles protected me—a concept that was foreign to me up until this point— but on the other, I felt strangely confused. It was the first time I had ever encountered a homosexual individual. I wondered if there was something about me that I wasn't seeing in myself. *Am I always going to have people to grab at me? Why didn't I recognize that this was a girl, and why didn't I recognize that she was being inappropriate? Does this mean that I'm a homosexual too?* All of these thoughts flooded my mind for days, but I was able to evade those emotions by distracting myself with my newfound relationships with my cousins.

My teen-aged cousins attended school during the day, and I often attended with them. I would leave in the mornings with them to pile into a tiny side car and travel to the nearby town. I was immediately fascinated by their school, as it was so different from mine. There were many things that were uniform (they actually wore uniforms, which was a new concept for me), but many things that were lax. For example, the teachers allowed a large portion of their students' days to be spent conversing with me, practicing their English. Again, I got the curious attention of the teenagers I was surrounded by, but I wasn't concerned. My cousins were extremely protective of me, and I soon was a part of their group of friends.

One of the teens, Eliseo, took a particular interest in me. He would stare at me with kind eyes but would oftentimes be too ashamed to speak to me in his broken English. I had learned bits and pieces of the language—enough to communicate basic information—and between the two of us, we muddled through conversations.

He did, however, write to me. He wrote me short notes and letters almost exclusively in English. In those letters, he explained to me how he was *owaw* (ashamed, shy) and how *maganda* (beautiful) I was to him. I felt so special each time I received one of those letters from this brown-eyed boy who was afraid to talk to me, but then I would wonder, *Does he really think I am beautiful?* I had never been called that by a boy—ever—and here was this boy right on the brink of being a man. He was tall and gentle and tan and beautiful, and he grew that summer in the heart of this small-town Mississippi girl through his letters.

There is such a great degree of romance in the written word. Just think of how God reached out to us to inspire the writers of the Bible. The entire Bible is not just our history; it is a love letter to us.

That summer Eliseo and I got to know each other through broken conversations, spending time together during breaks in and out of school, and letters. Being completely immersed in a different country and having exposure to different people was probably the best thing that could have happened to me at that point in time. Then there was the boy, and that certainly was a positive thing for a girl who believed that if people were interested in her, they wanted only to grab and take and tear down.

I was completely removed from the things that plagued me back home, but the things that continued to race through my mind at the time were far too advanced for an almost twelve-year-old. I remember looking at the video-tapes from that summer years later, and you could see it all over my face and in my eyes— a certain degree of sad-ness and evidence of a troubled soul that shouldn't have been there at that age. I had learned to sink inside myself for so long and overprocess my thoughts that the child in me was evicted too soon.

My birthday quickly approached, and my family had planned a huge celebration that started very early that morning. I was literally woken up before the sun came up by a couple who came to give me a personal serenade with their guitar. Then it was on to preparing food for the festivi-ties. I was in complete shock when my mother informed me that my beloved Wilbur would be roasted for my birthday celebration. I contested that they couldn't kill the only thing that belonged to me, but it seems that had been the plan all along. I hid in the house, but nothing could suppress the pig's screaming as he was being slaughtered.

My mother had another surprise in store for my party—the biggest cake I had ever seen. It was quite ornate, with multiple levels and a staircase between the tiers from which it appeared a porcelain doll at the bottom had just descended. It was a Filipino interpretation of a Southern belle, which I was not. It was an absolutely beautiful cake, but my Filipino family had no idea what my life actually looked like Stateside.

My guests began to arrive and included all of my local aunts, uncles, cousins, the friends I had made at the school, and Eliseo. One of the funniest parts of all of the videos from that summer was the camera panning across a room to where Eliseo and I were slow dancing, then, at the realization of what was happening, my mother physically breaking us apart.

The summer was coming to an end, and I had enjoyed the greatest adventure, the greatest escape. I was about to leave with a new appreciation for life. There *was* beauty in it. There *was* light at the end of the tunnel. There was a much bigger world out there. I had gained all of these lessons and also an appreciation for how very fortunate we are in America. Running water, electricity, indoor bathrooms—these things that we expect and take for granted—are privileges.

I also had the sweetest little romance . . . almost. After my birthday party, I was able to see Eliseo at the end-of-the-year school program, and then I rarely had the chance to see him. My little preteen heart was devastated.

I remember being so upset over not seeing Eliseo again as I spoke with my cousin at her mother's office. I was leaving the following day. My aunt's office was in a government building in the center of the town, overlooking the local basketball court. My cousin and I were talking about him, and then there he was on the basketball court—Eliseo. I had never thought I would see him again, yet there we were, in the same place at the same time. My cousin called out to the group of boys below. I immediately locked eyes with him, and my heart skipped a beat. We rushed downstairs, and a small group of my summer friends gravitated toward each other. My cousin and the outlying friends eventually drifted off as Eliseo and I walked toward the ocean. He probably spoke to me more on that one walk than he had the entire summer. He was no longer *owaw*, and as he spoke, it made me feel *maganda*. It was a beautiful afternoon, but the day was coming to an end. The barrier islands were tiny in the distance, and the sun was beginning its daily descent. As we walked along the bay, it happened. He kissed me. It was one of the most perfect moments of my life up until that point.

That summer was such a stark contrast to my life back at home; it was an escape in the most exhilarating form. I was someone else. I was someone that no one there had ever met. I was new to my family, and they wanted to know more about my life, more about me. What they didn't know is that I was hiding a very sad little girl. I projected an image of someone I wanted to be, and I could do that there. I could be anyone I wanted to be, and in that I learned more about myself.

When I got back from the Philippines, my father didn't recognize me. I was so sun-kissed that I literally walked up to my father and he looked over and around me. I had changed.

The next week when school started, my life was back to what it was before. I was still in the same small town where everyone certainly knew my secret. I was still silenced by my family. I was still stuck in a prison of a home that most parents did not want their child to visit. I began to write, and I wrote a great deal because of my lack of having anyone to talk to, especially about what had happened to me. I wrote letters, songs, plans for my future, poems. This was my therapy. I also read a lot too. I would often take out the same Bible that my aunt and uncle had given to me and read Scripture.

CHAPTER TWO

DAWN: THE SECOND TWELVE

Be sober, be vigilant; because your adversary the devil walks about like a roaring lion, seeking whom he may devour.

1 Peter 5:8 NKJV

The anger began shortly after, and the evil that I could feel within my home began to grow exponentially. My mother got angry at my father after the whole ordeal surfaced because he still continued to visit with my uncle, sit and talk to him for lengthy periods of time, and take him or his wife to the doctor—whatever they needed. It wasn't just my dad; all of my aunts and uncles catered to them.

I stopped going to family functions. It wasn't fair for me to sit across the table from him and be forced to look at him, was it? He couldn't look me in the eyes anyway. I was so uncomfortable and disgusted, especially when he was the one who was asked to bless our food. It hurt. I felt like I didn't matter. It hurt Tia too. We didn't understand. It was like they forgave him and my aunt too quickly for us.

I remember that my family convinced an impressionable Tia that she needed to forgive and forget without even fully processing what had happened. The neighbors pressed charges against my uncle, but our family did not, because family was the bond that seemed to be stronger than anything else, even if it was at the expense of the younger generation.

There were a lot of years of anger toward my father's family. I felt as if they were constantly beating me over the head with the commandment of forgiveness when I could not conceive of it. The concept of forgiveness was impossible; how could I forgive someone who had taken advantage of his relationship with me for years?

I could feel anger rise up within me every time I saw their house—a constant reminder. I also had anger for all of the other children it had happened to. I wanted to testify in court, but of course, my dad would not allow it, and that made me angry too. I wanted someone else to acknowledge me and what I had been through, but no one ever did. I dove deeper into my writing.

Examination

have you ever looked at your flesh and blood
and recognized . . . nothing . . . ?
no common purpose
or joy in tradition
or empathy
or love?
have you ever looked at your flesh and blood
and realized
your dark skin and
your dark eyes and
your dark hair are
paradoxically threatened
by their white name,
white skin,
white morals,
have you??
ever looked at your flesh and blood
and grown weary of comparison?
sometimes I wonder

did I make myself a stranger?

or did they push me out?

either way

no one is lamenting

There were a lot of things my parents never understood about me or themselves. The generation gap between my parents was a strain in and of itself, but the cultural and emotional barriers drove a silent wedge between them. The atmosphere was different in our home after the arrest. There were grudges held. My parents weren't getting along, and I wasn't getting along with my parents. To add insult to injury, there was the reminder next door; having to ride by their house every day was a constant, cruel reminder.

A lot of the tension in our home arose from the fact that my father would not speak about the situation with his brother. He didn't want to talk about it, yet he spent hours on end with his brother throughout the week. This hurt. I would come to recognize that I had always felt rejected by my father because he chose loyalty to his brother over me. He had always been a very distant father. Whether it was from his experiences in the war or the generational gap, he never truly cared to develop a meaningful relationship with me.

I saw this same pattern in his relationship with his eldest daughter, my half sister. I saw her a handful of times growing up, but I recall a period of what seemed like years that they did not speak to each other. She was twenty-five years older than I was, so forging a relationship with me was quite awkward, I'm sure, as she never was a constant in my life. I remember her reaching out to my dad when she hit milestones in her education, her career, her personal life—reaching out for approval that I'm sure she never received.

The Lord was the only one who knew my situation and the only one I could go to about it all. I needed a Savior, not only from my situation, but from the future I might have had. I needed a Father, because my earthly father was not the daddy that I needed him to be. *The Lord knew.* I was so hungry for a father figure, but I did not yet realize He had His hand on my life the entire time.

My Aunt Belle became sick, and when I was fourteen, she died. It was devastating to me, since I felt so much empathy for her. She lived her life terribly misunderstood, and in that I connected with her in a strangely similar way. I remember riding in the same car as Tia in the funeral procession line. It was a solemn ride, but she was about to reveal to me something that would make me see my Aunt Belle in a new light.

Tia told me that her father had revealed to her that Aunt Belle had been abused when she was younger by her brother (my uncle). Suddenly a million thoughts rushed into my head, and I saw her schizophrenia diagnosis with absolute clarity. It was cause and effect. My aunt could not handle the toll of the abuse; she literally was mentally broken. In a way, I feared the same fate for myself, but in that moment, I was so very thankful for Tia because with her I had an ally that did not exist anywhere else within our family.

On the other hand, I was angry. The abuse within my family had been covered up for years. The same person had caused so much hurt within our family over the course of decades; even more troubling, it was the same family that worked equally hard to cover it all up. All of this—all—was at the expense of children. *Am I the only one who sees something wrong here?* I pondered. I didn't understand how a family who purported such high standards, such high moral values, could completely ignore the fact that women and children had been abused for decades.

Every time I thought of my Aunt Belle after this, I thought about that car ride to her graveside service and the moment I found out why she had lived a life so broken. She lived the majority of her life institutionalized; he lived his life free. She lived as a prisoner of her own mind; he lived free to act out what was in his mind. I saw my Aunt Belle as a victim, but I also knew in her death she was free.

White

White is the smoke
That covers your eyes

White is the shame
You cover up with a shroud

White is the name
I cover up with a lie

White is blasphemy
For what is going on here

Its equivalence

Innocence
That was never really there

Whoever causes one of these little ones who believe in Me to sin, it would be better for him if a millstone were hung around his neck, and he were drowned in the depth of the sea. Woe to the world because of offenses! For offenses must come, but woe to that man by whom the offense comes!
Matthew 18:6 NKJV

As I mentioned before, I had felt uneasy about our house since I was a child. I never liked being alone there. There were so many bad memories attached to that house, and in retrospect, I always felt like there was something else in that house.

My mother and I began to argue on an almost daily basis. I remember several occasions when she would throw things—whatever was in reach—and once it was a brass candlestick. Tia was with me once when the object of choice hit my door as I shut it behind me. I learned to run pretty fast.

During another fight, she locked me out of the house and literally stood on the other side of the door, peeking out of the glass window in the wooden door, taunting me. She stood there like a child making faces—sticking her tongue out, rolling her eyes—and I was so enraged that I punched right through the glass window and lacerated my hand. It shocked me when it happened because I had no intention of doing that. It was ridiculous and mirrored the same level of inappropriateness as her behavior; however, I was still a child.

There was one day, though, that reached a whole new level of frightening.

I should stop here and mention that there was some use of a homemade device to contact my mother's dead ancestors within our home. I see now how easily evil was welcomed into our home, and if you aren't aware of how damaging dabbling in the occult can be, the Bible is abundantly clear on this matter (see 1 Samuel 15:23; Isaiah 8:19-22; Micah 3:7, 5:11–12; Galatians 5:19–21; Revelation 21:8).

So, back to the day . . . I do not remember what we were arguing about, but I remember standing in the hallway where it opened to our living room, where she was sitting. She began to threaten me with the spirit of her dead father. All of the negative energy in the house culminated in an all-out screaming match. At the height of our conflict, the most surreal thing happened all of a sudden. I don't even know how to accurately describe it, but I felt three knocks below where I was standing. Now, we lived in a one-story home, I was wearing shoes, and I was on carpeted floor. Nonetheless, it was as if I were standing barefoot on a piece of plywood and someone was underneath me knocking on the board hard. I started screaming and jumping up and down because it scared me so much, and my mother seemed entertained by this. The knocking was audible. It was one of the scariest things that has ever happened to me. After this happened, my mother responded with, "See? I *told* you so."

Chopsticks

she writes in capital letters that
look like chopsticks
and makes funny faces to make me mad
she cries when she misses me
and she blames me
for everything
but she doesn't understand
sometimes I think her pride
and her ignorance might weigh

her down one day and
just crush her.

but she wouldn't tell anyone.

Ironically, my mother considered herself a very religious person. She had begun attending Mass semi-regularly, and sometimes brought me along, too. I tried very hard to understand the traditions, the symbols, the pomp-and-circumstance way of conducting worship. I found myself looking at the beautiful building, windows, statues—everything within the building—but I couldn't find the God I worshiped anywhere. I never understood why my mother didn't feel she had direct access to God, as I felt in my heart that I could go to Him at any time with my pain. I was awkwardly uncomfortable when I went to church with my mother. I could not participate in Communion since I was not a part of the church. I didn't understand the significance of Communion at the time, but I felt like it was such an exclusive thing and I was undeserving. I remember being painfully aware that I was the only one in the entire church left sitting as the parishioners filed into a long line to the priest. I tried very hard to pray, but I didn't feel free to do so. My attendance at the Catholic church was short-lived.

As I grew more distant from my family, my need increased for close relationships. It was bound to happen at some point—I fell for a boy. The first time you fall in love, everything is all butterflies and shooting stars. Nothing is more magical than feeling as if you are walking through each day in a dream.

His family became my own. His mother had taught me in elementary school, so I was very comfortable with his family, whereas I felt like an outcast in mine. Being with his family was the first time that I had felt like a part of a family in years. He had no idea what I was going through at home. If he knew about my abuse, he never questioned me.

I started attending church with him occasionally - the first time I had been to church in years. Everything was perfect. There were roses, letters, and then there were the shooting stars. Oh, the shooting stars! Every night we were outside together, we would see one. There were countless perfect moments.

There were also the bad moments. One day as he was coming home from college, he got behind my best friend's car. She slowed down, and as he proceeded to pass her, she sped up. He tried to get back into his lane, but she wouldn't let him. By this time, a car was approaching in the opposite lane, and he had to run off the road to avoid a wreck. Thank God, no one was hurt, and it caused only slight damage to his truck. My best friend called me as soon as she got home (I suppose so I could hear her side first) and told me that he had wrecked. After hearing his side and the accounts of the two girls that were in the car with my best friend, it became clear to me that something wasn't right.

My boyfriend was perpetually jealous, convinced that there was someone else. There wasn't, but I had secrets I couldn't tell him. Not *that*. The tension of knowing there was something much deeper became palpable in our relationship. I felt like I couldn't ever be completely open and honest about my abuse. Eventually, I found out that my "best friend" had a crush on him and gave him room for doubt by the things that she would tell him. We finally broke up but crossed paths again in a year. For that year, I was a lost little girl. I felt like I had awoken to life and all its cruelties, but I could still remember a dream. He was the dream, and I couldn't get the dream out of my mind. After that year, I felt like I was drifting off to sleep again to continue the dream. Everything was perfect again, and then suddenly not. This pattern continued over the course of the next decade, not only with this relationship that seemed like a perpetual flame, but within other relationships as well.

I never told him my secret that I was still holding on to. I never told him how I truly felt about him either. We never had sex; that was completely out of the equation. No matter how comfortable I was with him, I never thought I would be able to go there with anyone. Besides, I knew in my heart those things were reserved for marriage.

It was around this time that I became friends with Josephina, or as I called her, Joey, a girl who moved to our school after her mother married a man not much older than we were. She and I became quick friends, and because her mother was so engrossed in her new relationship, we spent a lot of time together. I almost took on the role of a mother for her, and to this day, she tells her kids that I helped to raise her, since her mother was absent for so much of her life around this time.

One day one of my older cousins, who also happened to be one of the biggest advocates for keeping silence and order within our family, came over to my house. Now, this was something unusual, as I don't recall her ever just dropping in for a visit. She asked to speak to me in private, and I had no choice but to hear her out. She began to cry as she told me how her daughter had become pregnant in high school and was forced to marry afterward. I had no idea that this was how that relationship had transpired, but I was very confused as to why she was spilling her feelings out to me in such great detail and with such emotion, since she had never shown any real emotion toward me before. After she left my house, I began to process the conversation, and then it hit me: she had told me all these things because that was what the family assumed about me. They all assumed that I was carelessly promiscuous because of what had happened to me. I was confused. Sex was the farthest thing from my mind. In fact, I wondered how anything sexual could ever be a good thing. It seemed like it only wreaked havoc on life, and it disgusted me that I was conceived from an act of it.

That realization pushed me into another depression. If my family assumed the worst about me but was not willing to even address the worst thing that had happened to me, then what was the point? Why even worry with what they thought if they already thought the worst of me?

I found a network of friends with whom I could escape my house. I sank into a place of self-loathing, self-pity, and self-destruction. I began to drink, smoke, and even used marijuana a few times. I did these things to escape. I did these things to numb the pain. It was the closest I came to killing myself since the day I had contemplated it on the couch. I am so thankful that I do not have addictive tendencies, but I can see where my behavior could have derailed my life very easily.

That life was not life. It was checking out of life. It was escaping from life to go somewhere else—somewhere dark, somewhere that only flesh exists. I can tell you this from my experience: there was nothing productive or good or lovely about that life. *But God* . . . He spared me. He kept His steady hand on me although I was breaking His heart daily.

The thief cometh not, but for to steal, and to kill, and to destroy: I am come that they might have life, and that they might have it more abundantly.
John 10:10 KJV

During my junior year, I signed up for Allied Health. I knew that I wanted to go into the medical profession, and I also knew that if I was going to escape my town, I needed to start working toward making that happen. This two-year course played an important role in molding me into who I am. My instructor, a nurse, was instrumental in my decision to become a nurse. She also unknowingly provided an escape and support for me through the hard times.

My mom left that year on what was supposed to be a temporary assignment in Ohio to care for a lady who was wheelchair-bound. A friend had been caring for her but was about to take a lengthy vacation to the Philippines. It was timely indeed, her leaving. We really needed a break, since no one in the family was getting along. I remember watching the bus haul her away in the distance as I opened a card that should have been a birthday card. It was a sympathy card instead—a metaphorical slap in the face.

I gradually dropped out of all my extracurricular activities. My mom had previously helped me financially to do show choir, but my father saw no value in these things, so I could not continue. I tried to stay very busy going into my senior year. I worked, sometimes until midnight, and went to school. Looking back now, I don't see how I did it, but then again, staying busy was a way for me to relieve stress. Work and school consumed me and provided an escape that I desperately needed.

Joey and I continued to spend a lot of time together. One morning she and her mother stopped for breakfast as they were driving to school. As Joey sat there and ate, her mother got up and walked out of the restaurant, across and out of the parking lot, and into the woods. She was out there for hours until the search came to an end.

Joey never came to school that day. I was worried. Later I found out what had happened. Her mother was alive, but not in any state to care for her daughter, so Joey was to move back in with her grandparents in the town she was raised in.

Our friendship was a constant; now we were both left to deal with absentee mothers and process the accompanying issues related to that. She combated her sadness with faith; I was there the weekend she was baptized. Our friendship deepened, and we spent weekends and special occasions with each other. We were more like sisters than friends, and although we lived a few towns away from each other, people associated us with each other.

My mother came home, but it was only temporary. The storm at home raged now more than ever, and it became more and more apparent that we weren't going to be able to weather it. My mother left again, this time to stay with a friend. One day I came in from school and there was a stack of stapled papers on the table. My mother had filed for divorce.

I was torn; divorce had always been my greatest fear when I was younger. My mother would constantly remind me that I was the only reason she was staying behind. Her dream was to go back home, and she made it abundantly clear that I was the only thing holding her back—as if she were doing me a favor. I loved my family, but as I got older and those relationships crumbled, I was left with broken pieces of reality. Those broken pieces formed the kaleidoscope of my life where seemingly every turn created the illusion of something better, something right and true. Even with the falsehoods that existed within my family, hardly anyone in the family was divorced, so when I saw those papers there, it hit me hard. I felt responsible. I felt like a total failure. I was cursed with a hopelessness that I would carry with me for years.

My parents eventually divorced when I was a senior in high school. The divorce was long, drawn-out, and complicated. The day of the actual divorce, I was ready to get it over with. I was present, as the decision had to be made on where I would live. Of course, I chose my dad. My mother didn't have a place to live, as far as I knew, and at this time, she was back and forth to California, which is another long story. I was aware that she had also stayed at an abused women's shelter at one time. There were many times when I didn't know where to find her. At times, she would be in a hotel. At another time, she had begun to work in a local restaurant and had an apartment.

I was stressed and depressed. I had so many major life decisions as I approached my high school graduation, and my life was once again in shambles. I probably gained about fifteen pounds, sending my self-image and self-esteem further into the downward spiral. I had a string of empty relationships where I was physically present but emotionally unavailable. Against all odds, I was still making good grades in school, and I eventually graduated with honors. No one ever knew what was going on inside of me, save for one meltdown that I distinctly remember having in front of my allied health teacher.

Empty

we give our words existence
and put our faith therein
we give our hopes to falseness
and lead our dreams to sin
we cannot find the answers
to satisfy our hearts
we cannot see perfection
or break through life's ramparts

what are we without God?

Things were about to change.

I was still so angry—so very angry. I had walls up that no one could tear down. I had become jaded. I trusted no one. I was an only child who had grown perfectly content with being alone.

One day I was in our backyard, cleaning out our shed, going through my mother's belongings. My aunt and uncle's house was in plain view, as always—the constant reminder. He was home. I could see them both in the yard. I was going back and forth between the shed and the yard with boxes of my mother's things. I would see the house and get angry all over again. Repeat.

On this particular day, I was really wrestling with forgiveness. It was a thought that had, up until that time, been inconceivable to me, so the thought was absolutely not mine. It could have been planted there with such conviction only by the One who made me.

As I was opening boxes, I came across many items from my childhood: toys, books, dolls. I found crosses I had crocheted with my aunt, and then there it was—my first Bible. My heart began to soften. I heard a voice say to me, *"If it were not for them, you would not know Me,"* and I was immediately broken and began to cry.

The great I AM was correct: I would not have been introduced to Christ at an early age if it were not for them taking me to church on Sundays. I wouldn't have had the Word to read if it were not for that Bible. I wouldn't have had basic knowledge of who Jesus was and what He did for me if they hadn't taught me. In that cathartic moment, I instantly had an indescribable relief, as though the elephant that had been in the room my whole life sitting on top of me was suddenly gone. I forgave my aunt and uncle that day.

I saw things with complete clarity that day. I was a sinner and needed a Savior. All sin was disgusting in God's eyes; only in man's eyes are sins labeled in varying degrees. I could have gone the rest of my life hating my uncle, but instead, I chose to forgive him. God had forgiven me, and in turn I was given the ability to forgive my uncle. It might have been the hardest decision of my life, but it set me free. It didn't mean that I was going to restore contact with him and my aunt. It didn't even mean that I had to tell them. The forgiveness was not for them—it was for me, and for the first time in my life, I understood that.

But the Helper, the Holy Spirit, whom the Father will send in My name, He will teach you all things, and bring to your remembrance all things that I said to you.
John 14:26 NKJV

(on sublimity shared alone)

there's something about watching leaves fall . . .

(watching trees shed themselves of last year's burdens)
that makes me rid myself of fear
(I am no longer afraid)
there is such an incredible force of renewal
and energy
and life
and beauty
in such a moment as this.

(it's funny
how the simplest things
make me want to praise God,
but that's where I find Him—
in moments like these
that's when I hear Him—
in moments like these)

I am not afraid.

I prepared for college. I had gotten some scholarships but was still unsure of the path that I would actually take. It wasn't until the week before school started that I decided where I was going to go to school. Part of my moving forward with such hesitation was based in fear, but mostly I wanted to make the right choice. I have found so many times in my life that when I wait until the eleventh hour, God always comes through to take care of me.

In my first week of school, on a Wednesday, I got a phone call around four o'clock in the morning. It was my mother calling to inform me that she was leaving for California. It was a rushed move. She explained that her life had been threatened. She was leaving town within the next few hours. I had many questions, but I was too tired to completely understand what was going on, other than to realize that it was happening again: she was leaving.

I was still working the same part-time job I had worked since high school, and between driving to school and the job, I must have driven a hundred miles a day. It became more and more difficult to get up in the mornings. That first semester was very difficult. I made new friends, but I still felt empty. I began to have questions about God, and God, the amazing Provider, gave me a friend who answered all of those questions for me without me even asking her.

I started going to church again, this time with my new friend, and to a place where I was engulfed with love the minute I walked in. It wasn't long before I got involved in various ministries. I served as an assistant to my friend, who taught a group of preschoolers on Sunday mornings.

I eventually had to leave my job because of the hours and distance I was commuting on a daily basis. I found work at the college as a work-study student and soon became a fixture in the English department. Later I was asked to take on the role of editor for the college literary magazine, which I accepted. One of my greatest achievements around this time was our magazine placing second in the state competition. This was a time of much introspection for me, as my writing had always been personal to me, but on a spiritual level, I was seeking as well.

During the week, I attended a college-age Bible-study group at the local university campus where I would eventually transfer. On the weekends, I went to church and met with my small group for Bible study. During the summer, our church sponsored backyard Bible clubs in various local communities. It was a way to actually take the church into the community instead of having the kids come to church for vacation Bible school. I was asked to lead the crafting activities for the group that I was assigned to. The irony in this was that I had never attended a vacation Bible school as a child; this was my first. I was still a baby in my faith walk. I was learning alongside four- and five-year-olds in church every Sunday morning. In retrospect, God was once again giving me exactly what I needed. I was still on spiritual milk but was taking in small bites of food for my soul here and there.

During that summer of 1999, I joined my group of college-aged kids to bring the Word of God to our assigned community: a trailer park in the outlying rural area of the city. The community may have been rundown, but as a group, we created a kingdom that we had no idea would continue to live on in the hearts of those children. We dressed them as young princes and princesses, and I helped the children to craft sparkly crowns and banners. That backyard, for a week, was a safe haven for children, and it was completely transformed into something that it was not: beautiful and enchanted. That week was absolutely magical, and many of the children were led to Christ.

This is where I met nine-year-old Amanda and her siblings. Although it was hot, the children were dedicated in their attendance and seemed to grow in number over the course of the week. They seemed to enjoy how we related the lessons to a real-life fairy tale, and they giggled at the antics of the duke and the court jester. It was an oasis in the midst of the most dismal landscape, and we had no idea as teenagers what an impact our pretend kingdom would have on God's literal kingdom.

When I turned nineteen, I began to date a young man who was a year younger than I was. He began to go to church with me and became involved in many of the same church activities and functions that I attended. One night the Lord placed something on my heart that would change me. It was a prompt that I didn't quite understand, and I wrestled with it for hours. *"Tell him."*

I was so nervous that my hands began to sweat. I tried to remain calm, but the Lord's urging was even stronger. *"Tell him!"* This did not make sense to me and went against every ounce of my being, as I had kept my secret inside for all of these years and felt it was pretty safe there. *"Why, God?"* I asked, not wanting to comply. His answer was the same: *"TELL HIM."*

I started out with a nervous, "I don't know why I'm telling you this, but I feel like God is telling me to share this with you . . ." I fumbled for my words and danced all around my secret until I was able to get it all out. He began to sob, and then I began to sob. I was shaking;

I had never been able to open up like that to anyone, much less a boyfriend. I felt as if I had been in a fight. I was exhausted and broken, but relieved.

He then began to tell me how he had experienced a very similar situation as a child and also struggled with anger, hurt, and unforgiveness. I sat there amazed. It was perfectly clear to me why the Lord was urging me to talk about it now.

Over the years, God has urged me to tell countless people for no apparent reason, except that when I do, each individual has their own story of abuse. I can't tell you how many times this has happened to me, but I have found that when I am obedient to His urging, not only is the recipient blessed, but I am blessed as well. It's happened far too many times to be coincidental, and it's something that I could never explain. *But God . . .* God knew how to speak to my heart, and I cannot imagine how different my life would look today if I had not learned to listen to His voice.

That fall I continued to be involved in church, continued to work as a work-study student, and continued to work towards my academic and career goals of becoming a nurse. My boyfriend had become my best friend, and

I was so thankful for someone who understood a part of my life that could only be comprehended by someone who had also been abused. God was drawing me closer, and what happened next can only be accurately conveyed to you by sharing the actual journal entries from that time in my life.

Excerpts from Dawn's journal

October 13, 1999

I'm driving home with an overwhelming sense of depression. My little black cloud appears out of nowhere sometimes, a consuming sadness that is content with feeding on itself.

Though I am a Christian, I still struggle with depression, but it's not like it used to be. God watches over me constantly, lifting yokes I cannot bear, taking away burdens that I cannot remove in my own strength.

It's funny how music affects your mood and how your mood affects your music. I change the radio station in search of something—something somber, maybe. I come across a song I know. Something about it speaks to me:

the song is about letting the Spirit of God speak through you – through the words you say and your actions.

I had an hour test two weeks ago, one that I could have easily failed if I hadn't studied for it. The night before, I decided to skip out on studying and go to Crossroads at USM, a Christian group that is a ministry of my home church. I told God that He was more important than my test anyway, and that I was going to trust Him to give me the ability to retain the knowledge that I would need for the test (in college-student terminology, "cramming"). I am glad I chose to go. I love to worship, and He loves for me to worship. During prayer, I found myself repeating, *Use me, God; use me.*

God blessed me with a 98 on that test.

I set my alarm for 9:30 a.m. *I'm giving this to You, God. Thank You for taking on my burdens so selflessly. Amen.*

October 14, 1999

My mind's eye opens to a world I have never seen, but what I see gives form to a presence that is so familiar.

I am not afraid. He is on His side, His torso a mountain upon the horizon—an alp that no human could scale or even begin to fathom. I can barely see His left arm; I suppose it is there. I conclude the obvious, the truth that I have always known, that the rest of Him exists even though I cannot see it. Behind Him, there is sky; in front of Him, a burning fire, a refining fire that changes our lives, burns away the past, and brands us as His children.

I stand at a great distance from Him, but He is larger than life, surrounded by people the size of ants. I cannot see their faces. I'm not the same size as the Lamb or His people. I'm just a spectator at a distance. Then He turns and looks in me. I say "looks in me" because He knows me better than I know myself; it's not like a human being looks at you.

His visage is my joy, even though it reads suffering and sadness. I cannot remember if He moved His lips, but I could hear Him clearly: "Will the people walk with Me, or stray away from Me?" Then His gaze shifts to His left.

I turn to see this woman. She, too, is larger than life. She is absolutely beautiful, with long, dark hair that she coils above her head. In her eyes, there is a lure for deceit. She is the evil that exists in many forms. Her name is Lust, and she represents misplaced desire for cars and clothes and fame and fortune. I see that many people also surround her. She is the focus of many who turn away from Him.

I wake up to a clock that reads 9:31. My alarm should have awakened me a minute ago, but I discover that after

I set the alarm last night, I forgot to turn the thing on. *Thank You, God, for waking me up!*

It doesn't really occur to me what just happened, and then I start to remember. It hits me. I begin to fully wake up, and I lay there contemplating the vision and its meaning for ten minutes.

I begin my drive to school. I'm alone and thinking of the vision that God gave me. I'm praying and praising, and in this moment, it's just me and God. I'm driving over roads that are covered by trees on either side – like a tunnel. The leaves are beginning to turn. The trees are giving up pieces of themselves from last season that have now turned golden, and one by one, they fall into my path like glitter – a beautiful show just for me, from a loving Father God.

The same song I heard yesterday begins to play again, and the realness of what I had seen strikes me anew. I begin to find more and more meaning within the vision. I wish I had stayed home to write it all down.

It is so hard to hold back tears when you have been touched so deeply. I can't concentrate at school; I find myself enmeshed in the same scene over and over again. I've told three people so far, and they were all touched with its message.

On the way home, I ask for more. I find myself listening to silence, begging for His voice. As I drive through my small town, I see an old black woman walking on the side of the road. In her left hand, she trails a tall white bag full of aluminum cans; in her right, a brown paper sack. It's getting late; something tells me to turn around and give her a ride. Then something else within me rises up to say that I have too much to do—I need to get home, I need to do this, I need to do that. Besides, I don't want all that stuff in my car. Immediately I hear the voice that I've been begging to speak: *How do you expect to touch people's lives if you don't show compassion?*

The song floods my radio once more, and in this moment, I'm reminded of just how real God is, and I'm so thankful for the life He has given me. This song is the cry of my heart.

Lord, help me listen to Your voice. Help me to silence that voice that rises up within me, the voice that is characteristic of me, not You. I pray for more of You and less of me. Let my life be a reflection of Your love, and let my love for people have no eyes. Let it be an unconditional, blind love that You shower us all with. I pray for those who do not know You. I pray that Your good news will be heard by all people groups, and that You will begin to work in the lives of those who have developed hardened hearts and deaf ears to Your Word. Use me, Lord, to spread Your Word. Let Your Spirit speak through me in times when I am without words. Help me to incorporate the vision You gave me into my life, and give me the opportunity to touch the lives of others with it. Thank You, Jesus, for being my burden-bearer, my friend, my Lord. Thank You for giving us all the opportunity to have eternal life. Thank You, God. Amen.

It wasn't long until the winds of change began to blow about in my life. It was time for changing, for growing. My faith was going to be tested.

My father and I remained in the same house where I had grown up. I had some things happen to me during that time that stay with me to this day. I remember very distinctly that there were occasions in which I woke up and felt like someone was pinning me down. In my mind, I was absolutely awake and lucid, but I could not move. I was not dreaming. I felt like I had a blanket of a person over my whole body, holding me down so hard that I could not even move my eyelids. I would tell myself, *Move your arms, open your eyes, do this . . .do that...*, but I couldn't do anything. After a few minutes, instantly it was gone, and I could sit up, scream, and fight back. However, for those few minutes, I was paralyzed. It felt like a very specific attack that was meant for me.

After those attacks, I would scream for my father. He would come into my room, puzzled. I tried to explain what I was experiencing, but alas, he could not protect me. He had never been able to.

A year and a half into college, my uncle became terminally ill. One morning at breakfast, my father, who up until this point had never acknowledged the abuse, said to me, "I think I know why they never had children." It was the first hint of validation my father had ever given me that something was not right with my aunt and uncle. That was it, though—nothing else. I wanted more than just that simple statement. Nineteen years of nothing and then I get this one blip? No! I wanted an explanation, an apology—something.

It was then I realized I had not forgiven my father.

I tried to ask questions, but he would not answer. I resorted to picking a fight with him to try to pull something—*anything*—out of him, because he would not even acknowledge me. My persistence got me nowhere. *You think you know why they never had kids? You think he was afraid he would do it to them, too?*

68

I was so angry I could not focus on anything else during the day. This one-sided conversation carried over into the next day until finally—and I will never forget the moment—I provoked a response, but not the one I expected. My father looked at me and said, "Well, what did you expect me to do? He is my brother!" I looked at him with tear-filled eyes and said, "And I am your daughter."

I went on to school that day. My father had pierced my heart with his words, and I was bleeding on the inside. My chest began to hurt. That night I started to have the overwhelming sense that I was surely dying. Looking back now, I know I was breaking. Heartbreak can cause an array of psychosomatic symptoms, and I was at the age where I could have definitely taken a turn for the worse and suffered the same fate as my Aunt Belle. This was what she must have felt, holding on to the anger toward our family.

At some point during the night, I called 911. A local first responder showed up within minutes, then the ambulance. I remember sitting in the back of the ambulance, crying. I looked at the paramedic and told him that I could no longer live there. He didn't ask any questions; he just assured me everything would be fine. He had no idea what kind of storm was raging internally.

I was transported to the local emergency room, where I was promptly unloaded and the judgment from the team of nurses and doctors began. I don't even remember anyone speaking to me directly; no one made eye contact. They spoke in circles around me, but no one really cared why I was there. I was a waste of space in their emergency room. My father had basically just told me that I was worthless to him. He confirmed with words what I had felt in my heart for years: a confirmation of my insignificance. I was broken, but there was no earthly medicine that would fix the deep wounds inside—wounds that no one could see but I could still feel.

I moved out of my father's house the very next day. I found the first available apartment and moved in as soon as I could. It wasn't in the safest part of town, but I didn't care. My father's house was no longer safe.

After I moved out, I no longer had any of the episodes where I felt like I was being pinned down. I didn't have to fear the house I grew up in. I no longer had to pass by the house next door. I was free.

It wasn't long afterward that my uncle passed away. He had a celebrated life by some; he was hated by others. He left a legacy of a road named after him—the road sign of which was regularly spray-painted over or torn down in the nineties—and a string of broken girls and women who carried the hurt he inflicted over so many years.

When I found out that my uncle had died, I wasn't happy, but I was definitely not sad. I honestly didn't know what to think or feel, so I did what I knew best to do at the time: I picked up a pen and paper.

Not an Elegy
There's a certain degree of joy in your death
The one who tormented me for so long
Unknowingly
The one whose demons paid homage
Daily
I can't help but wonder
If you're scared
Scared that your obituary might mention
What you were
There's one look I could give you
After I tell you I have forgiven you
It's not one of grace
Or sadness
Or pity
It's a look that says
I wish you could have died content with your life

It wasn't long afterward that my relationship with the boyfriend that I had first opened up to fizzled out. There was so much healing in that relationship, but our time was up. We were both still young and were moving in opposite directions. The relationship served its purpose. Seeds were planted. Lessons were learned. I mourned the demise of our relationship for a while because he was the friend that God had given me at the perfect time in my life—the person who shared my same pain in a way that I had not been able to share with anyone else.

Upon a cold living room floor

upon a cold living room floor
a pale-pink blanket
wraps around my body
(a cocoon)
but this pale pink blanket
where he used to be
is just another barrier
and he's grown weary
he scales the wall
but he knows
he can't make it this time

revelation time:
"we're not right
for each other"
he sees the look and he knows
that i know

he knows that i've known
he asks me how long
and his world falls apart

he is like a newborn
all that he has known to be true
curdles like milk

his living room
becomes a morgue
pale-pink blanket
becomes a body bag

i close my eyes
because i've already faded
i close my eyes
because it still breaks my heart
to see him
cry

i am like a newborn
all that i have known to be true
sets me free

pale-pink cocoon
opens
i spread my wings
because i know how to fly
i spread my wings
because i've already flown

Around this time, a few major events happened: I started dating my best guy friend, Samuel, from high school, and I was accepted into nursing school at the university I was attending. I moved into another apartment in a safer area, and this time I needed a roommate. One of the girls who was in my nursing class was looking for a roommate as well, so we moved in together.

I should say here that I never expected or planned to ever date my friend, but one day Sam was in a horrific car accident on the way to school and nearly died. He was transferred two hours away to a medical trauma unit, and I went with a group of friends (ironically, my last boyfriend, the one I had spilled my heart out to about my abuse, was in this group) to see him in the hospital. When I walked in and saw his broken and bruised body, his tracheostomy, and his bloodshot eyes, I just wanted to take care of him. Part of this was me still trying to figure out my emotions, but the other half was the nurse that was growing within me. After Sam came out of the hospital, we were pretty much inseparable, and the relationship that ensued seemed to be a natural sequel to the feelings that had been blooming between us.

I had never been a girl with a ton of "girl" friends. I always had one or two friends that I would stick to, but this changed when I was in nursing school. I had a group of girls that I became close to who became lifelong friends. One friend and I had actually known each other since elementary school; we had taken the same path with our prerequisite courses and were also accepted into nursing school with each other. Then there was Elizabeth.

The roommate situation declined very quickly. She had a questionable relationship with a boyfriend; from the outside, there seemed to always be a lot of fighting. Then one night he called me to tell me that I should come pick her up. I left our apartment to head to his, and when I got there, I was overwhelmed by the number of emergency vehicles present. I circled around until the police cars and ambulance left, then caught him outside to ask him what had happened. The girl apparently had broken through a glass window in his apartment.

When I arrived back at my apartment, at least part of his story was corroborated by the amount of blood I found on the door, the walls, the phone, the floor, the countertop—blood was everywhere. A police officer brought my roommate home and she had gone to bed by the time I arrived. I spent half the night cleaning up the apartment. After she started to skip out on payments and a few checks bounced, I had to tell this girl that it was time for us to cut ties. This was a nightmare of a life that I didn't want to live in. I had run so hard and distanced myself from my family to find some sense of normalcy, stability—and now this. The girl ended up moving out and eventually dropping out of nursing school.

With the vacancy, I needed another roommate to fill the space and help with bills. This is when Elizabeth moved in, but not without hesitation. She had heard both sides of the story with the previous roommate and was not sure which roommate was truly the mentally unstable one. I may have been a bit unstable at times, but I was always able to disguise my inner struggles because I was strong. I was high-functioning in my struggles. Some may humorously say that I was able to "hide my crazy." Nevertheless, this sorority girl moved into my apartment, and my life was changed forever.

She became my very best friend as we spent nearly every waking moment together. We lived together, we went to school together, we studied together. She had an incredible faith that inspired me and a confidence that I lacked but so desperately wanted. Above all, she was loyal, and she was constant. She fought for me when I was unable, advocated for me when I could not speak or others wouldn't listen (she later would beg my own mother to agree to attend my wedding), and has been an ever-present force as a voice of reason in my life since those days in the old apartment.

When I was in my early twenties, Sam and I went to the local courthouse in the town where we grew up to try to get an understanding of what had happened in my uncle's case. I asked for the case files and was able to read through my uncle's psychiatric evaluation, which was interesting to me at the time since I was in nursing school, as well as the court records. From what I could gather, the case was moved to another county so he could get a "fair trial," because everyone locally knew about the case.

I found a conviction of "child abuse," but I also found a statement of nolle prosequi on the child molestation charge. These words stood out to me as I read: *guilty, plea, misdemeanor.* Then the confusion set in. There was a conviction. There was a jail term, but it was suspended. The terms and conditions were not a charge at all. He got to live out the rest of his life in peace—because the court deemed it "fair."

The most distracting and disturbing thing was reading about myself. I was floored when, as I was reading, I found my name within two separate testimonies by both another abused victim and her mother. I was never questioned by anyone, and yet there was my name, staring back up at me and anyone else who could access the file. My heart pounded in my chest. My mind was full of questions. How many hands, how many ears, how many people knew about these documents? How did something so highly publicized fall by the wayside, and how were the victims passed over, as if we were "lesser"? It was abundantly clear to me that things were as I had always suspected: the adults were very aware of what was going on but chose to say nothing.

This day unraveled whatever healing had taken place thus far. Every page that I read ripped the scab wide open and left me vulnerable to the infection of anger, hurt, and confusion. I had never felt so insignificant. All of these children had a chance to tell their testimony in court; yet there I was—the girl who lived next door, the niece, the daily visitor—and no one even cared to ask me, in public or in private, if I would tell my story. I began to feel as if my story didn't matter, but deep down I knew that was a lie from the pit of hell. This was just another layer of my story, and God was building and growing it daily.

The Lord had a plan much, much larger than I could have ever imagined. He still had His hand on my life. He was still in control, and He was steadily writing my story.

As nursing school came to an end, so did my relationship with Sam in a very dramatic and traumatic way, which is where I found myself so often. I never allowed myself to fully trust a man, and in that I could not be trusted. I sabotaged many relationships when I felt as if I were being hurt or I was close to being hurt. I self-destructed before someone else had the chance to destroy me. This was a protective mechanism. Some animals have shells or quills; I was deceitful in a way that hurt others and me.

During this time, I also strayed from my faith. I used lack of time and school as an excuse, but I soon found that the more I was out of church, the easier it became not to go. If no one held me accountable, I could not do it by myself. I was still stumbling around in my walk with God and had no real direction because I wouldn't stop to listen. The only person who held me accountable during this time was Elizabeth, and it wasn't her job to carry me. That was Jesus, and I wasn't allowing Him to.

After I graduated from nursing school, I could have moved anywhere. I had considered it for so long, but I didn't. I sought multiple opportunities to work in various emergency rooms, but it seemed that no one was hiring, especially not a new graduate. So I prayed and then prayed some more. I had no idea where God would lead me, but I knew He would, and He did.

We have divine appointments on our journey in life, and my getting my first job was no exception. You see, I had not even filled out an application, nor had I been formally interviewed. I simply toured the hospital, but when I met the nurse manager for the department, I found the emergency room had no job openings. When I received the phone call from human resources weeks later, I was surprised. Then, when I found they had done their research to find me, I was even more surprised. Taking that job set so many things into motion that simply would not have been had I moved across country and started over.

As a brand-new nurse in a high-stress environment, it naturally brought me out of the shell that was comfortable for me. There were many nights that I slipped away to cry in private, almost like a rite of passage. Death and trauma made me become tougher, and the challenges of fighting for my patients enthralled me. During those years, I worked night shift and learned just about more than my heart could handle about the nature of people.

Emotions are always at an all-time high when people come to you at their all-time low. I often thought of my ambulance ride to the emergency room in college and how far I had grown out of that girl. I loved being on the other side, but it was also easy to become jaded there, especially when you were verbally or physically attacked. I remember being kicked, pushed, fussed at, and cussed at. I was never wounded physically, thank God. I was generally able to handle the verbal abuse until one night a lady called me something that cut right to my core: *yellow girl.* She meant it intentionally, and I suppose she thought that this was going to help her cause, whatever it was.

It was easy to get jaded in that environment. I definitely had to find ways to decompress. I still wrote, but not as often as I did when I was younger.

Yellow Girl

Never seen anyone
mixed like me?

Do our differences scare or intimidate you?

It's true:
I'm not like you,
And *that's so relieving.*

The summer I turned twenty-four, I traveled back to the Philippines to visit my family. I was once again welcomed with open arms, and I had another incredible summer of adventures. During this trip, I documented my travels through photos, and my scrapbook from that summer is still one of my prized possessions.

It had been twelve years since I had seen my family, and it was quite a shock to see how much my cousins had grown. I had grown too; I was no longer the little girl who desperately needed an escape from her reality back home. I had a life; I had a career. I was in a completely different place than I was before, but still searching for purpose in my life. Change was once again on the way, and I had no idea that by the end of the year, I would meet the man I would marry.

Gradually Becoming Blonde

I am the girl who confuses those
Who present to me with what matters most
(Is this really the most pressing issue to the world?
"Can I ask you a question?")

I am a hybrid,
A half-breed,
Is that what you want to hear?

The answer is always the same
I feel like I have no place,
Past a question-mark-face
I feel like I have no name.

My Filipino family calls me *Fil-Am*
They say I am *maganda*
And teach me how to do things,
Like pick up jellyfish
And carve fruit into art

My White family *never calls* me.

I never realized how different I was
Until I felt more at home

In a place that was not my home
Who knew that attempting to assimilate
Would be such a paradoxical thing?

Gradually becoming blonde
Americanized as can be
I took my soul upon a walk of possibility

Afraid of who I am
Exploring all of me
Searching for a way to change
My dual-ethnicity

Braid the hairs of who you are
To create your soul and find
Something more permanent:
You've made a stitch in time

CHAPTER THREE

DAWN: THE THIRD TWELVE

O God, You have taught me from my youth; And to this
day I declare Your wondrous works. Now also when
I am old and grayheaded, O God, do not forsake me,
Until I declare Your strength to this generation, Your
power to everyone who is to come.
Psalms 71:17-18 NKJV

I had been set up on one too many blind dates, and
I was completely over it. I was asked once again
about meeting someone. I said no, so this man found
out where I worked. He asked his cousin's wife about me
because he knew she had worked in the same place, and
it turned out that I had trained her. He was persistent.

Eventually there were phone calls and a blind date.
Six months later, Corey asked me to marry him. We

planned an October wedding, and less than two months away from our wedding date, Hurricane Katrina struck the Gulf Coast.

At the time, I had just moved into a mobile home that Corey and I would share. I was still working nights in the emergency department, and our management had advised us to stay at the hospital, but I declined, instead choosing to sleep at Corey's parents' house. A few short hours later, it started raining. Then the wind picked up. Then the roof was peeled back, and it began to rain in the house.

That evening after the storm calmed, I had to go to work, but there were trees down everywhere. Corey and his father loaded up in Corey's big truck to take me in, and along with their chainsaws and the help of neighbors, we drove through pastures and over and around downed trees. When we absolutely couldn't get by, they cut a way through. It was dark, but we could still see destruction everywhere. My usual fifteen-minute drive turned into an hour and a half.

When I got to the hospital, it was chaotic, as expected. I found out the man who had just made my engagement ring had lost his life in the storm. So many people were injured. There were so many challenges in lack of resources and being cut off from the world, both at home and at work. We had no power, no cell phone service, nothing. Travel had to be limited because gas stations were completely depleted of gas, and when you did find a gas station that was up and running (usually with one or two pumps), it was not unusual to wait in line for an hour or more.

This literal storm was a metaphor of the years that were to come. The first years in my marriage were very challenging; however, as Corey and I grew in faith personally and together, we were able to weather the severe storms of life.

My father had declined to the point where he had to move into a nursing home. This was extremely difficult for him since he had been so independent for so many years, but he had become unsafe at home. He was becoming increasingly confused and eventually was diagnosed with Alzheimer's disease.

I had distanced myself over the years not only from my father's family, but from my father as well. I had to. I had heard my father tell me "You'll never amount to anything" one too many times. I always knew the drive, determination, and purpose that I had within me—something that no one in my family seemed to see, including my father. Then there was the day he told me I didn't matter at all, especially in comparison to his relation-ship with his brother, which stuck with me for years. I had not forgiven him. Distance was not only healthy, but necessary.

My half sister and my father's niece—the cousin who was always adamant about not speaking out about the abuse, the same cousin who came to my house when I was a teenager and tearfully told me about her disap-pointment in her daughter's teenage pregnancy—became actively involved in pursuing power of attorney over my father. The cousin had outright told me that I had a responsibility to step away from my life and take care of my father, but I just couldn't. I instead chose my life with my husband and my career.

The cousin was still harboring animosity toward me all these years later, except now she had a different weapon. She was happy to become overly involved, how-ever, so I allowed her to take on the daunting tasks that I didn't have time for. I remember at one point I found myself alone with her in a car as we were moving my father's vehicle, since he was no longer safe to be on the road himself. I took the opportunity to initiate a conver-sation just to tell her, from my adult perspective, how she and the other adults had made Tia and me feel as kids. I should have known better. Nothing constructive could ever come from this. She still saw me as a child.

She cut me off in the middle of what I was telling her and said, "You need to get over all of that. That happened a long time ago!" She did not realize that in that one statement, she stripped the wound of its scab.

Before my father was placed into long-term care, he was in a unit for geriatric patients as the doctors tried to get his medications regulated. When I visited him there, it was the only time that he was ever confused about who I was. As I sat there talking with him, he confused me with someone from his past, and at one point, I think he thought I was his other daughter. I wasn't sure about some of the things that he was telling me, so I reached out to my half sister.

It was around this time that I was able to see her occasionally. One day I was able to spend a whole evening in Chicago with her while I was there on business. It was really kind of amazing to both of us how many similarities we had. We both had the desire to advance in our careers. We were both strong and independent. We both had an affinity for paisley patterns. We both had a strained relationship with our father.

When I asked her about the confused conversation that I had while visiting our father, she told me about the woman that my father was speaking of. It was a woman that my father had left her mother for. She also told me that after their divorce, he actually came back at one point and remarried her mother. I had never known that he married her twice. It made complete sense to me at this time why his ex-mother-in-law was never fond of him.

She also told me an account about another woman—a woman who lived in my hometown, a woman whose house I would trick-or-treat at as a kid and would occasionally visit. Apparently, when my half sister's mother and our father were newly married, this very pregnant woman threw herself across my father's car and exclaimed that he was the father of her baby. When asked at the time, he denied it and said the woman must be someone who was crazy.

My half sister and I had many conversations over the next few years that would shed light on so many questions that had previously been left unanswered. These discussions eventually led to me telling her about my abuse and how our uncle was eventually arrested. She had never been exposed to him or abused by him as a child and had limited knowledge of the whole situation.

My dad began to contract pneumonia on a regular basis, complicated by years of smoking. Eventually the doctors found that a tumor had wrapped itself around his pulmonary artery. When he was hospitalized, I would get off work in the mornings, drive to see him at the hospital, drive home, sleep, wake up, and go to work. Repeat.

One night as I sat in triage, I felt the strongest conviction to share the message of salvation through Jesus Christ with my father. My father had always had a hardened heart, and I wasn't sure if he would hear what I had to say. When I got off work, I headed off to see my father and placed a call to Corey on the way. What he said hit me in the stomach and gave me the confirmation I needed. He said that I had to witness to my father about Jesus that day, or he would do it himself. He explained he had stayed up all night thinking of this one thing.

When I arrived at the hospital, my father lay there so still that I had to wake him to make sure he was still alive. He no longer had the tall, strong frame that I remembered as a child. He was no longer mobile. He was frail and childlike.

February 23, 2006
An e-mail to Elizabeth:

> *My dad's in the hospital, and he's not doing very well. Today was actually a better day than yesterday, though. He was actually talking this morning (too weak yesterday),*

and when I walked in, he said, "Dawn, where's my car?" (He hasn't asked me about it in months; he used to be so preoccupied with it). I was actually able to feed him today; yesterday he was so weak he couldn't suck through a straw. If only you could have seen him yesterday morning—it was awful. I worried all night long at work that I'd get a phone call telling me to come in, and then I started to worry that I hadn't talked to him about Jesus. Then, on the way to Collins, I was talking to Corey, and he said he couldn't sleep because he was thinking how I needed to ask him, and that if I didn't do it, he was going to.

But the best thing, the strangest thing, the thing that has given me so much peace, is this: My dad had always shunned or pushed me away or changed the subject whenever I tried to talk about this. As I was sitting on his bed, he looked at me and said, "Dawn, will you tell me when it's time for me to go?" I said, "Daddy, it's time," and then I started talking to him about God and what Jesus did for him, and if he believed that. I asked him if he understood what I was asking him, and he said "Yeah, but I don't know how to answer that." I told him all he had to do was believe it and say he believed it. It didn't cost a thing, and everything else in the past didn't matter; all that mattered was this. Then he said yes, indicating he understood. I asked him again, and he said yes, so I asked if I could pray with him and he said yes, so I began praying. I opened my eyes in the middle of my prayer and he was looking up, all around the ceiling. I prayed for angels to surround him in his room; I prayed for forgiveness and healing.

Today was the best day I've ever had with my father—ever. It was nothing short of a miracle.

That next January, I received a phone call in the middle of the night that my father had died. I was honestly quite surprised by how I handled the phone call. I had lived so many years without this man. I faced loss of life almost daily in my career. I knew my father had accepted Jesus as his Lord and Savior, and I had forgiven him of all his shortcomings that same day, but here I was crying, hyperventilating. I was in no shape to drive, so Corey came to the hospital and picked me up as we drove to the nursing home in the middle of the night. I will never forget the image of his tiny, lifeless body lying in his bed. I leaned over and gave him one last hug, and the pressure of my body on his caused the shell of him to exhale one last breath.

Dad

There are only tender thoughts now
No more anger, or hurt
No more tears

This is how I remember
Dad, who insists on using the same plate on every trip
to the buffet line
Who points with his middle finger and
Tells embarrassing stories about his youth
Who hates war movies
But thinks of The War every day
Still fighting battles in his mind
That I could never win for him
Dad, who is convinced that the sun rises in the West
In certain places like the Philippines
And will argue you down about it

Until the last cigarette . . .

I wonder what life would have been like
If he hadn't fathered me at sixty-four
Quite ordinary, I suppose

At our father's wake, my sister and I encountered many people who were fixtures in my father's life at one point or another, and some that we had never met before. There was the man my dad always played poker with, the sheriff who was always a friend to him, the host of aunts and nieces, and then there *she* was.

I had not seen the woman since I was young enough to trick-or-treat at her house. In light of our conversation, my sister and I were acutely aware that the woman she had with her could be his daughter, our sister. My cousin introduced the younger of the two to my sister and me, and the three of us stood in an awkward circle and just stared at each other. When we finally spoke, I can't remember the words that came out, but no one asked "the question." After they left the funeral home, my sister and I agreed that the lady looked more like our father than either of us did.

The Beginning of the Bad Dreams

Wednesday, March 14, 2007

I dreamed that I was reliving my father's funeral again, except things were a lot different.

In my dream, the funeral parlor was different, and there weren't many people around. I really don't even remember any specific people. There was one heavyset man who worked at the funeral home, but I didn't know him. I remember him briefly; it seems he was there for the sole purpose of opening the door and showing me to where my father was. I didn't see him, but it seemed to me that my husband was at my side the whole time. I don't remember even seeing his face, but I could feel his presence.

When I walked into the room where my daddy was, he was lying in his coffin—as frail as he was while he was sick, skin and bones. However, he was alive.

He was talking to me, and it seemed like I was the only one who could hear. I remember being so confused. He told me that he had been dead when he was in the morgue. In my mind, I had a picture of a typical made-for-TV morgue: a large room, cold, dark, and full of large stainless-steel drawers to hold bodies. He said that when

96

they pulled him out of his drawer to place him into the coffin, his body had warmed and he was alive again.

It's like a saying we have in the emergency room: you're not dead until you're warm and dead. This is derived from the fact that humans, especially children, after perhaps a submerging incident where they were in water for a while and became hypothermic, can sometimes be revived after the body temperature returns to a normal range. It's likened to a state of hibernation.

In my dream, my father, who was so frail and weak he could not even move his small frame inside the coffin, was alive and coherent and talking to me. I don't remember much about anything else that was said. I remember having the impression that after the wake that night, they were going to return him to the same cold morgue, and he would be dead again for the night.

The next day, the funeral day, I remember going to the same funeral parlor with the same heavyset man and the same room, and Daddy was again alive inside the coffin. I remember feeling at that time more confused than ever. If he was alive, then why were we burying him? Again, it was as if I was the only person who could see these things. It made no sense to me whatsoever, but I was still going through the motions of his funeral. I remember my father not really verbalizing any uneasiness about the whole situation. It seemed like I was the only person who thought the whole situation didn't make sense, yet I didn't point this out to anyone in my dream. I didn't tell my husband, and I didn't tell my daddy. I didn't say anything.

I never did see the casket close in my dream. That was it, and I woke up not remembering I had even had the dream.

That night, a Wednesday, Corey and I went grocery shopping, and when we returned, I walked into our house, into our bedroom, and something just did not feel right. It seemed like when I looked at our bed, all of a sudden, the memory of the dream flooded my mind, and I remembered going to sleep that day and the dream I had in its entirety. I walked back through the house and into the kitchen, all the while reliving the dream in my mind, and I was suddenly just paralyzed with emotion. Corey was still outside unloading groceries, and when he walked back inside, he was puzzled as to why I was crying.

Crying is an understatement. I was sobbing hard like a child, gasping for breath just like I had the night my father died when Corey picked me up from work and drove me to the VA home to see him, just like I had when I woke up after he had died, just like I had while I was shopping for the clothes that he would be buried in and called my sister to tell her I had found the nicest paisley tie—just like now, as if the dream had come back with a vengeance and knocked me square in the face with itself.

March 22, 2008

I woke up screaming this morning.

I dreamed that I was at my dad's house. I was standing in the backyard using a water hose to spray down this slant of dirt by the house that was eroding away from under the house. All of a sudden, a huge snakeskin washed out from under the house. I turned around just in time to see the tail end of a snake slither back under the lid of the propane tank. I started screaming, "Daddy!" at the top of my lungs. I kept screaming, but he couldn't hear me (of course not, Dawn, he's dead). In my dream, he was alive. I never saw him but knew he was there.

The snake reappeared. It came out from under the lid headfirst, looked right at me, and started moving toward me. I continued to scream for my dad, this time asking him to bring a gun. I've never seen a snake like this before in real life. It was light brown, black, and a brown that was almost red. It looked like pure evil. It scared me when the snake started moving toward me, so I sprayed it with the water hose. This really made the snake mad;

he seemed to leap from the propane tank to the ground and began to chase me.

That's when I woke up, still screaming for my dad. My heart was beating so hard and so fast I could feel it in my throat. It almost hurt.

I woke Corey up. I felt really silly yelling out for my father like that.

The next day, I told Corey I wouldn't go there by myself. We went to Daddy's house to work on it. I found myself standing, at one point, in the same exact spot where I had the snake encounter in my dream. It was a strange feeling, like déjà vu.

I painted the bathroom white and found myself trying to "white out" memories instead.

Healing has been a lengthy process, and I'm still finding healing and forgiveness. I now know that I don't have to try to go it alone. I eventually found that family is sometimes the friends, coworkers, and church members who surround you. As far as forgiveness for my relatives goes, I have forgiven them, but I have no relationship with them. Forgiveness does not equate with reconciliation.

Healing has also come into my marriage. I don't think I'm alone when I say that if you have been sexually abused, there are unique and challenging circumstances you face in your marriage. Intimacy can be a struggle, especially if there are triggers that occur through any of the senses that bring back bad memories. It takes a lot of patience and understanding on the part of the non-abused spouse who hasn't experienced the trauma and pain of abuse.

It has taken Corey and me years to get to where we are, and there are still times that we have things to work on. It has not been an easy path, but without God in our lives, there could have been times that would have been very bad for us. I am so thankful that God has had His hand in our marriage and that we are in the place we are today.

I also have found so much healing through being a mother. As a child and a young woman, I was always afraid of what kind of mother I would be. I didn't know if I was capable of becoming a good mother. I was also afraid of having girls—afraid of the world and afraid of what I would do if the world hurt them.

Today I can say that Corey and I have been very blessed with two precious little girls who are not only giving, loving, and respectful, but who also love the Lord. Most days they completely get it: it's all about loving and helping others. I am amazed over and over at what God has provided. It's almost like God is telling me, *Remember all those times you cried out to Me as a child? Here you go. Here is your do-over.*

Every now and again, I find myself in a rare situation where I am around someone from the small town I grew up in, and I am referred to as my uncle's niece. It brings about a sense of awkwardness and shame; I still battle these feelings years later. There is a certain stigma that comes with being labeled my uncle's niece, but in my heart, I know who I am. I am saved by grace and the blood of Jesus Christ. I am a daughter of the most high King. I am free, no longer bound by the chains of depression, shame, and darkness.

When I think about how my relationship with Jesus has evolved, these verses are the cornerstone of my faith: "And we know that all things work together for good to those who love God, to those who are the called according to His purpose" (Romans 8:28 NKJV); and "'For I know the plans I have for you,' declares the LORD, 'plans to prosper you and not to harm you, plans to give you hope and a future'" (Jeremiah 29:11 NIV). I did not think there was hope or a future for me; as a child, I could not see how He was working in my life. My life could have been much, much different today, but praise God, He saved me!

The healing from sexual abuse is a process. Even though you may have forgiven your perpetrator, it's quite difficult to forget. Talking about it helps tremendously. I would like to help others who feel alone in their situation; I remember how bound I felt all those years before I was able to speak about it. I really believe this is a form of ministry that God has laid upon my heart.

My story is about God's grace and how my Savior is truly my Father, my rock through it all. My testimony today is about how thankful I am for the Lord's presence and protection in my life. If you, too, have been abused, you do not suffer alone. God is real, God is big, and *He hears your prayers*. He wants to change your life, your situation, and your story. He knows the plans that He has in store for you (Jeremiah 29:11). He does not want you to do anything alone, and if you listen to the still, small voice within your heart, you will find His Spirit guiding your heart (John 14). Trust Him and trust His promises, for His Word *never* returns void.

If you would like to be free from your past – a past full of hurt, disappointment, shame, regret, just know that you are never beyond the point of salvation. Jesus Christ came so that you could have abundantly blessed life, but the enemy will always try to get you to believe that you have no hope, which is a lie (John 10:10). If you would like to have a personal relationship with Jesus, and you don't understand how, let me share with you. It isn't complicated. The first thing you need to do is very simple. You pray. Don't know what to say? I'll help you. There is nothing magical about this prayer, but if you are sincere, and you truly believe this with your whole heart, you have received salvation: *God, I'm coming to you now because I have nowhere left to go. I'm tired and I can't go on any further. I want to be free, and I want to know you. I'm a sinner in need of a Savior. Lord Jesus, I believe with my whole heart that you died on the cross for my sins, and I thank you for it, Lord. You are the only way to eternal life.*

If you just prayed that prayer, and you sincerely want to live this life, please find a local Bible-believing church, surround yourself with people who will lift you up, and get into the Word of God. It is the best instruction manual on how to navigate this crazy adventure we call life.

CHAPTER FOUR

DAWN: THIRTY-SIX

✦

When I was a child, I spoke as a child, I understood as a child, I thought as a child; but when I became a man, I put away childish things. For now we see in a mirror, dimly, but then face to face. Now I know in part, but then I shall know just as I am known. And now abide faith, hope, love, these three; but the greatest of these is love.

1 Corinthians 13:11–13 NKJV

At the beginning of my story, I mentioned my epiphany on my thirty-sixth birthday. Thirty-six just felt *different*. I'd like to elaborate more about that here. My first twelve years, as you have read, were lost in mixed messages about life, love, spirituality, and innocence spent far too soon. For the next twelve years, I was left to interpret the mess that was made and learn to channel my anger into something—anything—productive. My twelfth birthday was marked by my first trip to the Philippines, and my twenty-fourth birthday was marked by the same journey; yet at thirty-six, there was no trip. I was more distant, literally, from my Filipino genes than I had ever been. I felt alone, but at the same time fulfilled. I had grown up. I had come into my own, but there were no flashing lights signaling that I had arrived.

The most important lesson I've learned this year, beyond forgiveness, is that not everyone is going to be for you, not even family; but if your family can't be your tribe, you have to plug in and find some people who will. Find a group of like-minded people who challenge you. Find a life-giving church where you can join small groups and flourish. We all need human connection; this is an integral part of the Great Commission.

Regarding forgiveness, I sometimes get unexpected reactions of shock and disbelief from various people who know my story when I tell them I have forgiven my family. I want to assure everyone that forgiveness does not come easily to me, but the forgiveness that I have does not come from me. It flows through me, *but* it is directly from God. Jesus Christ died on the cross for me to live my life in love, not in hatred, bitterness, and anger. I will say that sometimes an old memory or an old hurt will sneak up on me, and anger, bitterness, and hatred will rise up within me; things long forgotten tend to be used as a tool of the enemy. In those moments, I have to stop, refuse to react, pray, and forgive all over again. Healing and forgiveness happen in onion-peel layers. I'll discuss this further later on.

This year, I must admit, I am in a place in my life where I am truly happy. God has instilled *vision* into my life that has produced in me a vision of my *purpose* in life. From this, I have derived true happiness, and true happiness comes only from the One who created life. The most amazing thing about the way I felt about turning thirty-six was that it was only a glimpse of what God had in store. It was a reflection of how far He had already carried me, unbeknownst to me. I had no idea how much He had been moving already this year and how much He was about to move.

And ye shall seek me, and find me,
when ye shall search for me with all your heart.
Jeremiah 29:13 KJV

February 2016. I was restless. I felt stuck. I knew I had something inside me that I needed to share with the world. I had begun to take an introspective look into my life and found the testimony within my heart. God had been growing it there, watering it with living water (see John 4:7–14) and turning it into something beautiful. During a Bible study, I scrawled this prayer down as fast as it came to me:

> *Lord, I know that You can turn our tests into testimonies, our messes into messages. I have known You my whole life. You have had Your hand on my whole life. Thank You! Show me where You want to use me. Open doors. Put people into my path to facilitate Your plan. Mold me into who I need to be to touch the lives of others. Show me, Lord!*

I became pregnant with this prayer. It was a reflection of where I was in life. I was ready, I was willing, and I just needed Him to lead the way. Little did I know, God would begin to set things into motion—unimaginable things— that He would reveal to me a short nine months later.

In June, the company where I had worked for eight years was gearing up for an office move. It was a long, difficult process to comb through, consolidate, trim down, file away, and pack up the accumulation of stuff I had acquired over the years. It truly was a reflective time, and I likened it to life. We do this so often, and sometimes it takes years to process, understand, forgive, and take away life lessons from what we have been through.

In the midst of the moving process, our company was also going through some staffing changes. Hiring licensed practical nurses (LPNs) was a new practice for our company as a whole, because traditionally, we had staffed only RNs; however, having LPNs on board was our new normal.

On the day of our big move, a fresh-faced young lady in blue scrubs showed up at our office. At first, I thought she was there to market a service, but my manager soon introduced Amanda as our new nurse. She watched as chaos unfolded around her—movers hoisting huge metal filing cabinets and heavy cardboard boxes onto dollies, others breaking down desks with electric drills—and I saw that she looked slightly like a deer in headlights. We all made a collective joke that this sure was a way to start off her first day, but we soon found that she was quick and willing to jump in and help, hauling, in her own car, computers and boxes and whatever else needed to be moved.

Amanda was a brand-new nurse, having worked in a clinic setting for only about six months. It was easy to see why my manager had hired her. There was just something about her—a light, a spark, something. You know, when you meet someone and they seem to have a light that surrounds them? This was Amanda. I knew immediately she was someone who could be trusted, someone I could be friends with. Over the course of the next few months, I found Amanda to be very bright; she was keen to detail, quick to learn, and intuitive.

In November, I invited Amanda and her two boys to our home. Our four children together ranged in age from four to seven. She showed up on a Saturday morning, and the kids quickly became friends. Our girls hurriedly took their new playmates outside to play on our swing set, which allowed us privacy and time to talk.

Amanda started out with a question. She explained that what she was about to say sounded crazy, but she wanted to know something. "Do you know where Glendale is?" I told her indeed I did and began to explain how to get there from the interstate. Working in home health, I had grown quite accustomed to explaining locations of local communities to our clinicians.

She interjected, "No, I know where it is. Did you ever go to church there?"

I was confused. "No."

"Did you ever do a Bible school there?"

I hesitated, and then the summer of 1999 flooded my memory. "Yes, I did. I did a backyard Bible club in that community."

Then Amanda said something that changed the course of events forever. "I have always wondered if you were the same Dawn from back then."

CHAPTER FIVE

DAWN: PEELING THE ONION OF FORGIVENESS

For if you forgive others their trespasses,
your heavenly Father will also forgive you.
Matthew 6:14 NKJV

I have not always been able to tell my story from a place of healing. My healing has happened in onion-peel layers. It has been messy, stinky, and downright gross at times. In fact, the week that I invited Amanda over to my house, I had just reached a place of forgiveness for a cousin.

I had always harbored ill feelings toward this cousin since I was young. She was probably in her forties around the time my uncle got arrested, and in my mind, she was the leader and face of the movement to cover up any transparency about the abuse within our family. She repeatedly spoke to me about forgiveness at a time that I could not fathom it, and she used the Bible as weaponry instead of in love.

The Bible points out that love will cover a multitude of sins (see 1 Peter 4:8), but part of this message was lost on my family growing up. It seemed to me as if all of the adults within my family were very quick to forgive and move on, never acknowledging what had happened or that how I felt mattered. As an adult, I had good intentions of having a productive conversation with this cousin about the ill effects that her behavior had on me as a child. She was quick to interrupt me and let me know that she still did not want to talk about it. Her response was, "That was a long time ago; you need to get over all of that now and move on."

On October 22 of last year, my husband and I were leaving home to celebrate our eleventh anniversary. We stopped at the end of our driveway to get our mail, and I was shocked when I saw a card addressed to me from this cousin. It had been almost a decade since my father had passed away and approximately the same amount of time since I had last heard from her. In the card, she told me to stop by if I was ever in town, and she would love to see my family. Even though this cousin did have a purpose in contacting me (she was forwarding something addressed to my father), it really took me by surprise, and it forced me to take a long, hard look at my heart and recognize the feelings of unforgiveness that were rising up within me.

Our pastor once preached a sermon on forgiveness, and the message included a statement about how forgiveness does not equate with reconciliation. This one statement was so poignant, so freeing. I no longer had to carry the guilt of being an only child and not providing my children the extended family that so many other children have.

I was torn on whether or not to respond but felt in my heart that I should, because I needed her to know that I had forgiven her. After about a week, the words for a response began to flow. I let her know that I appreciated her thinking of me. I let her know that I respectfully declined her offer to reconcile, because as a mother, I had a responsibility to protect my children. I told her all the harsh truths that I had never been allowed to say in the conversation years ago that came abruptly to a halt—how I was left to feel voiceless, powerless, and condemned as a child. I then went on to say:

> *I am no longer bound by the labels, assumptions, and accusations of your family; I am not what you all assumed I would turn out*

to be. I am a daughter of The Most High King, and I am free! I give honor and praise to God for the way my life has turned out. It was a very dire situation at eleven years old when I cried out to Him and seriously considered suicide, but He heard my prayer and has been there as my Father, protector, defender, encourager, and friend. I have seen miracle after miracle in my lifetime, and He has brought me life and blessings through friendships and relationships that are closer than family. I am truly humbled by His blessings, His provision, and His purpose for my life. I pray that you all have a very real relationship with Jesus, because the time is very near. Lastly, I want you to know that I forgive you. I forgive you for the things you have said, assumed, done, and accused me of over the years—all of it.

The Sunday after Amanda came over, I was talking to God as I unloaded the dishwasher. The conversations that I have with God when I'm doing the most ordinary of things are pretty amazing. I was praising Him for showing me how a Bible school held in a trailer park seventeen years earlier had made a difference, and processing how intricately He had worked out the details to bring Amanda back into my life. I had the sharp realization that this was all nothing short of His hand, His work only.

I was praying and praising—praying for guidance because I knew that what was happening was big, and praising God because He was much bigger. All of a sudden, the image of the letter I had sent off earlier that week flashed into my mind, and then I heard Him, the still, small voice inside me say, *Do you see the doors I can open for you when you allow forgiveness into your heart? Do you see this thing I have done?*

What kind of doors can God open for you today?

AMANDA—INTRODUCTION

*W*e all know that movie scene—the one where the little girl in the white cotton dress is swinging under the big oak tree. Her long, wavy hair is blowing in the wind, and her eyes are bright with the wonders of the world. She doesn't have a care in the world, and why should she? She's only a child, and to be a child means to be innocent. It's a nice fantasy, really, one I often go to when I get in my own head. My childhood, however, I can assure you was no fantasy. It was in fact a living nightmare, and my monster was very, very real.

Now before I go any further, let me say this: What you are about to read is an unfiltered account of what I went through. If you are looking for a pretty, painted picture, you won't find it here. This is the raw, ugly truth of what I experienced. I want you to understand what I went through so you can see where God brought me from. As you read these words, know that they come from the deepest place of vulnerability. The next chapters are a combination of a time before I knew the Lord and after I accepted Him into my life. As you will read, I write from both perspectives.

You see, I grew up in a home with a stepfather who did not believe in Christ, and in turn, neither did we. It was not until one summer in 1999 at a backyard Bible Club . . . but I'm getting ahead of myself. I have struggled with where to begin because I was left on repeat for so long, like a broken record, day in and day out reliving each moment. So, I will start here: I am Amanda. I am twenty-seven years old, a survivor of sexual abuse, and God is my Savior.

CHAPTER SIX

AMANDA: THE BATTLE

"In the same way I will not cause pain without allowing something new to be born," says the LORD. "If I cause you the pain, I will not stop you from giving birth to your new nation," says your God."
Isaiah 66:9 NCV

I am the oldest of four kids, ranging from two to eight years in age difference. I have one brother and two sisters. Growing up was difficult because I spent most of my days tending to my younger siblings. I'm sure that most older sisters take on that role, but I was babysitting, cooking, and cleaning as far back as I can remember. Don't get me wrong—this has helped me in my adulthood. Becoming a mother was a lot less of a shock for me because I was . . . well . . . prepared. I loved those three little monsters with every ounce of my being. I was their big sister, their protector, their friend. I didn't realize then how far I would go to protect them—not until the abuse began.

From the moment you came into my life
I knew I'd always fight for you

When the storms come rolling in and the bullies
knock you down
I will fight for you

When the invisible monsters wreak havoc on your life
I will fight for you

When the nightmares come back to claim victory
I will fight for you

When you give up on the battle and you lose your will
to carry on
I will fight for you

In hopes that one day I will fight *with* you

My mother was married to her high school sweetheart, my stepfather at the time; he was the biological father to my two sisters. He had always portrayed himself to be a likable person, someone you wanted to be friends with, but once you saw his temper, you wanted to cower away in a corner. For as long as I can remember, I had always known this man to be my daddy. He raised me from the time I was a baby. My biological father was not in the picture. I have heard different stories as to why my father was not in my life, but none of them made a difference. He was absent. For many years, I held a grudge against my biological father for this, but I found forgiveness and got past the jaded view on the matter. Unfortunately, it took a diagnosis of cancer and some disturbing facts about some things he had battled in his own life to bring me to that forgiveness and a relationship with my biological father.

My stepfather raised my brother and I as his own. Many told me, "He would never hurt your sisters—they are his *real* kids." What was I? What was my brother? Were we just strangers living under the same roof – cast aside for his own personal amusement? It made me so mad to hear that. How could someone decide to hurt a child, or children for that matter, and say, "Oops, not that one; we are related." I strongly believed, growing up, that statement was a way for the grownups to cope with their fear. I guess part of me believed it too, because I wished it to be true every night in order to protect my sisters.

You don't know him like I do
You haven't seen him through my eyes or felt him
through my skin
You don't know him like I do

Don't get me wrong—my childhood was not complete doom and gloom. I have some amazing memories, though they seem at times diminished by the dark shadow cast by my stepfather. I cherish the few bits of happiness I encountered as a young girl, moments when time stood still and I could focus on the "now." I loved playing outside on our swing set. I could be anyone I wanted to be, and I never wanted to be myself. I was an explorer in an enchanted cave, and I had to rescue my brother from "the monster." At other times, we would all play "Goosebumps"—at least, that is what we called it. We would just run around in the dark, scared of the nothing that was chasing us. We would play with our plastic dollar-store dolls; my doll's plastic counterpart was not good enough, so I chose my brother's rugged army men, and it made my brother livid. I would spend hours creating immaculate houses to spend five minutes playing in, because it was an escape from my reality. I also made the dolls be intimate with each other, which should have been the first clue that something was not right, but no one noticed.

Looking back now, I realize that every game we played was in one way or another related to running for our lives from this unseen evil or protecting each other from an invisible force that was meant to harm us. None of the games were ever pretend for us, and when I had a moment to realize I was having fun, I would stop—stop playing, stop pretending, stop fantasizing about what I wished life was like—because in my heart I knew that this was our real life, our reality. We never wanted to be who we were. We created elaborate profiles for each other, and once we decided we didn't like something about our characters, we simply changed who we were again. My brother would always say, "Pretend that my name is Mickey Alex." This made me laugh then, and even today it brings a smile to my face. He created this alter ego. Mickey Alex was the person my brother wanted to be.

My brother was the cutest little boy ever, with white-blonde hair, the brightest blue eyes, and the biggest cheeks any kid could ever have. As he grew into the man he now is, everything became dark. His hair lost its luster, and his eyes didn't shine as bright. My Mickey Alex was destroyed, and I miss him so much.

I am burdened with an image in my mind of someone walking down a single path that ends in two separate directions.
On the left is a beautiful meadow, and on the right, the same path as the one they are on already, maybe a little darker and less appealing, but still an option just the same.

The left, although it's beautiful, I know represents satan and his enticing sin. The path just to the right is God's way, full of its own twists and turns placed strategically as a challenge for its explorer.

I thought this image was meant for someone else. It wasn't until the next day when I received some devastating news that I realized it was meant for me—as a premonition of what was to come.

Suddenly the image replayed in my mind, only this time it had changed. Pan out and I see the bigger picture. Two people travel this path now, hand in hand. They are afraid—afraid of the path they are on—one boy and one girl running for their lives from the demonic figure that is sending them towards their hidden destination.

Which path will they take?

As they draw closer to the divide in the path, I realize the people in my vision are you and I. This path is a representation of our childhood.

To the left is the meadow. It's calm, peaceful, safe. It intrigues you. You are drawn to it, and sadly, I understand why. The path I choose for myself is the path to the right. I don't know why, but the safety of the meadow scares me. I don't know peace—I never have, and neither do you.

I reach out to you as I take a step towards a new future. "I can hear His voice telling us to trust Him," I say. You can no longer hear me. You release your grip on my hand and tell me to let you go—it calls to you. I watch as you are enveloped by satan's trap. He has you now. He gives you what you think you need because he's drawing you deeper into hell.

I watch. I mourn who you could have become, who you can still become. I am comforted by a mighty arm that holds me and whispers for me to pray for your sake, and that one day you will hear His voice and come to find His path. I travel this new route, and while it still has some potholes along the way, they help me become stronger. I am so strong now—strong enough to fight for us both—and I will fight. I will pray, and one day you and I will be hand in hand again.

Like I said, it is hard to look back on the good because it reminds me of the bad. To be completely honest, I don't remember much of the good, anyway. Even before the sexual abuse began, my brother was physically, mentally, and emotionally tormented by my stepfather. One memory in particular haunts me. We were in the car on our way home, and my mom and stepdad were trying to have a conversation. My brother and I were being too loud. My stepdad yelled at us to shut up so they could talk. My brother and I had these little inside jokes; they were silly and childish, but they made us laugh despite ourselves. One joke was what we called "Captain Crunch." We would salute each other, and then as we ended the salute, we would dramatically hit ourselves between the legs and in a long-drawn-out way say, "Captain Crunch . . . ouch!" while we grimaced from the fake pain we had inflicted on ourselves. I did this and made my brother laugh. This set off my stepdad. He reached into the backseat and grabbed my brother by his throat. His head fell into my lap as his face turned blue. His eyes were wide with fear, and I could see the small capillaries burst in his eyes. My mom called my stepfather's name to stop him, and he finally released his grip on my brother. He nearly died that day, and for weeks afterward, he had marks to prove the abuse. No one noticed until a few weeks later.

We were in a restaurant one day during those weeks that followed, and a waitress noticed the marks on my brother's neck. When she asked what had happened, my stepfather was the first to reply, saying he was just a typical little boy, and brushed it off. When he went to the buffet, she came back to us and told my brother if there was something he needed to tell her, he could. He was so afraid. We all were. She was a stranger in our lives, yet she was the only tiny hope we had for someone to know our struggle.

It's infuriating to know that out of all the adults in our lives, not even one noticed the clues, and the one adult who did know what we were living in did nothing about it. I assume this was out of fear, because my mind cannot fathom any other reason to watch a child nearly die at the hands of their spouse. This was a daily thing for my brother. One time my brother was throwing a fit about something. My stepfather put him in a diaper, gave him a pacifier, and made him go outside for our entire neighborhood to see "the big baby." My brother must have been at least eight years old when this happened. A grown man humiliated him. The scars he left my brother with are deeper than anyone can imagine.

We witnessed the abuse on almost a daily basis. None of us knew what to do. We were so afraid of him. My sisters, at the time, were young; they were too little to feel the full impact of what they witnessed. They remember bits and pieces of what my stepfather did to my brother, but not like Mickey Alex and I do. Even though we were seeing the abuse, he still had this way of making the good moments good. He would "make up" for what he had done by playing with us or taking us somewhere fun. As children, he knew how to play on us to make us forget what was happening. This really laid the foundation for the sexual abuse I encountered because he used these same techniques to entice me into doing what he wanted.

My mother ended up leaving and going to New York one day. She was gone for about a week. I didn't know why she left at the time, but I would soon find out. My sisters and brother took turns sleeping in the bedroom with my stepdad that week, and it was finally my turn. This almost felt like a treat for us because we were never allowed to sleep in the bed with our parents. I was so excited, although I had no idea of the horrors to come in the next few hours. I remember everything in such detail that when I close my eyes, I am forced back to that time and that place.

Earlier that year for Halloween, I was a witch, and my mom made my costume out of a black T-shirt that belonged to my stepdad. She cut the bottom so that it had little fringes, and I loved it so much that I kept it as a play shirt. The night that I was to have the sleepover in Daddy's room, I wore this to sleep in. We all went to bed like normal, only I was sleeping in my parents' bedroom alongside my stepfather. I woke up that night with my stepfather on top of me, lifting my nightgown to expose my developing breasts and asking if he could remove my underwear to "give me a kiss." I did not understand what was happening. It instantly felt wrong, and I began to cry and asked him to please stop. He began to plea with me, saying, "I need this; she left me," and he started crying. Suddenly I was filled with guilt. He was hurting, and this would make him feel better. Everything in my body wanted to run and hide, but I felt defeated and knew that whether I gave him my blessing or not, he was going to do this anyway; and I was afraid of what he would do to me if I didn't comply.

129

He performed oral sex on me that night and rubbed himself against my private parts while I lay there—unclothed, vulnerable—in front of him. I have tried for years to forget the images that play in my mind of these encounters, but I cannot. I remember every unwanted detail of how it felt . . . of how *I* felt. He cried afterward as I told him it was okay. I wanted to disappear. *I* was the one he had hurt, yet I had to comfort *him*. Watching him cry after every encounter became a normal thing from that point forward. He would cry, apologize, and then threaten my life or my family's lives if I ever said anything. I believed his threats. I knew firsthand what he was capable of. Fear was my new best friend. I lived the rest of my childhood in complete fear of this man.

I never slept in the same room with him again, but it was not my last time to be forced into the bed with him. That was the last night I saw the world through innocent eyes. I knew he was a monster when he was causing my brother harm, but now I was exposed to the world of sex at such a young age by this monster. I was told by my stepfather that my mother had left him for another man who lived in New York. I was so afraid she was not coming back, but she did, and life continued as it did before, only this time our family had a darker secret. My mom did not find out about that night or any of the others until a few years later. Later I was told a different reason about why she had left. She told me that she left because they got into an argument and he choked her. She said, "I started to black out, and I was so afraid you kids were going to walk in and find me dead. I guess he realized what he was doing, and he let me go and started apologizing and asking if I wanted to call the police."

As time went on, he got braver and found a way to touch me inappropriately while she was home, knowing I would not speak out or fight him. My cries were silent, and even though I wanted to say something, who was I going to tell? Now let me stop here and say this: I know this does not portray my mother in the best way. I have struggled with mixed emotions my entire life concerning my mom—heavy emphasis on the word *struggled*. Please note that now I am in a different place with her. Everyone has a chance at redemption. I love my mom, and while I may not understand her reaction or lack of reaction to the abuse, God understands, and that is all I need.

One night I woke up with a terrible cramp in my calf muscle. I thought I was dying. I had never experienced a cramp before and was scared, to say the least. I carefully and painfully made my way to my parents' bedroom for help. I wanted my mom but got the unwanted assistance of my stepfather. Suddenly my cramp was insignificant as I was shoved against and bent over the computer desk in our living room. He rubbed himself against me and fondled my breasts while whispering obscenities into my ear. I hated this man. He made my skin crawl, and I wanted to be as far away from him as possible. Every time he touched me, it set my body on fire with fear and pure hatred. Each time I would beg and cry and plea for him to stop, but my cries always were ignored.

I can recall only one time that he hurt me out of anger. I was playing with a toy, and my baby sister was driving me crazy, trying to take my toy from me. I got angry with her, shoved the toy in her direction, and yelled at her. Before I could even realize what was happening, my step-father reached down, grabbed my right shoulder, picked me up with one hand, and then, as hard as he could, shoved me to the ground. My baby sister cried because she was afraid, and all I could do was lie on the floor in pain, afraid to move from fear of something being broken.

Our entire life at this point was spent walking on eggshells, afraid to move, speak, or even breathe too loudly. My brother had already started to get into trouble in school and show signs of problems at home, but no one cared to notice. They all just thought he was a troubled boy. I remember him going to the juvenile detention center in Forrest County when he was in the first grade because he was stealing prizes out of the treasure box in his classroom so that my parents would think he was being a good boy and be proud of him. When the teacher and my parents found out, instead of investigating, they just took him for a tour of the juvenile detention center to scare him. Even as a little boy, the adults made my brother feel like he was the problem, when he was really crying out for help. He made many trips to "juvi" after that. He was medicated and turned into a zombie with medication for ADHD and behavioral problems. One night he completely panicked because he "saw the clowns on the wall moving." He was referring to the glass clown masks and figurines our mom had displayed on the wall. He was so medicated that not even his thoughts were safe from being tormented. I remember him going to a facility when we were younger, and to this day, I do not know if it was for counseling. He didn't get counseled well, if it was.

The abuse carried on, and life as we knew it went by one unpredictable day at a time. As I mentioned before, we were not raised in a Christian home. My stepfather was an atheist, or so he claimed, and the only time I went to church was when I went to visit my grandparents in Louisiana. They were Catholic, and I was christened in a Catholic church as an infant when my mom was married to my dad. Even so, I only got to see my grandparents once a year during the summer, and we stayed almost the entire summer. It was amazing—no fear, no looking around the corner. I could sleep, be a kid, and so could my brother. My grandparents had no idea of life back home. While we were there, our stepfather was the farthest thing from our minds. Life was perfect in this boot-shaped state far from the terror that lived in Mississippi. The only trouble we had to face while at Grandma and Grandpa's house was which rock-and-roll T-shirt we were going to steal from my aunt to sleep in for the night. The only monster to fear was the tickle monster and which face she was going to give us: marshmallow face or piggy nose?

Returning home was always a dramatic episode. How could we possibly return to a nightmare after living in a dream for two months? We always did, though, and life always picked right back up where we had left it. As a personal note to my Louisiana family, you guys will never fully know the impact you had on my childhood. I cannot thank you enough.

One summer we were blessed with a new adventure. We got to attend our very first backyard Bible club. Some teenagers from a church came to our rundown and less than ideal community to spread the word of Christ. The theme was "God's kingdom." They did an amazing job making everyone and everything look like an actual kingdom. We made royal-purple flags and ate cheese and grapes. It was incredible. I had my first encounter with God that summer, and it was brought to me by a beautiful princess named Dawn, the daughter of a King—a King I never knew existed.

Most little girls grow up wanting to be Cinderella or Snow White. Not me. Dawn was the princess I wanted to be when I grew up. Now, if you know Dawn, it's not hard to understand why I wanted to grow up to be like her. She has such a presence about her that's calming and nurturing. I think I honestly saw that in the short week that I knew her. I could also see God's grace all around her. God loved her, and in no way could I have ever known she herself was living through hell. Most non-Christians say things like, "If God was real, then why would He have allowed you to live through that?" Now I just introduce those folks to the book of Job.

The week went by in a blur, and we were so hungry for God's Word. This Bible was a story we had not heard before. It seemed like a fairy tale to us. When Bible club was over, I thought I would never see Dawn again and life would return to its usual torments. Unbeknownst to me, God was just setting a very incredible testimony into motion.

At some point amid our chaos, our parents decided to move away from the trailer park that we called home and into a huge brick house in a nice community. No more sharing a room with my two younger sisters. No more potholes in the dirt road. No more rundown, rusty old trailer.

I had hope, for some reason—hope that maybe when we started this new life, my stepfather would change his ways. This was a false hope; the move just revealed more depth to the evil that was my stepfather. This picture-perfect, all-American family had the darkest secrets. What seemed like new hope quickly became a worsening reality. I would come to miss the small space in the rusty trailer park and the potholes. The only great thing about the new move was new friends. One girl, Ann, became one of my lifelong friends, and I did not know it at the time, but she would play a huge role in the big reveal of my abuse.

As the days passed by, the abuse continued, but life became a little more bearable. I stayed the night with Ann almost every night, so much so, that her family became my family. We shared each other's clothes and were practically inseparable. We spent almost every weekend at the local skating rink. One night I wanted to go skating with Ann and my junior high boyfriend. My stepfather would "groom" me by stating if I performed sexual acts on him, then I would be allowed to go. When I refused, he forced me to perform the act on him anyway. Later that same evening, he decided to let me go skating and taunted me with statements like, "Are you going to have sex with him? You can—I won't tell your mom," or make comments about me French-kissing my boyfriend. I was so sick from the earlier events that I could not even speak to my date that night.

All the while, no one knew of my home life. I never let Ann stay the night with me, and when she would ask, I would come up with some excuse as to why she could not. I was safe in her home and felt that if she came to stay at my house, I would be putting her at risk. She would always ask to stay, and I would always come up with a new tale. The conversation never ended, and she pushed the issue until one day I finally caved and let her stay the night with me. That night I was on edge, more so than usual. Fear was a normal for me, but now I had to be afraid for an outsider. What if he tried to hurt her? What if I lost my best friend? I guess she could tell I was edgy because she finally asked the question I had been dreading since we became friends: "How come you never want me to stay over here?" Just like that, my whole world was about to change.

I didn't even give myself a chance to think about it. Before I even knew what was happening, I told her *every-thing*—every encounter, every emotion, every fear. It was as if someone had unlocked Pandora's box and all its contents were spilling out without any way to stop it. I cannot remember much of the conversation after that or her reaction to the truth she had just become aware of. A few short weeks later, my stepfather came into my room one morning before school and touched me inappropriately while I was getting dressed. This was nothing unusual and seemed to be part of a daily routine. A lot of times, he would just stand there and touch himself while staring at me as I was unclothed and sobbing. Other times, he would force me to do stuff to him or try to force himself onto me.

The hardest part of telling my story is the details. I want you to truly understand the horrors of my past so you can feel the full impact of how the Lord turned it around for me, but many of the details are too much for even me to handle. Like I said before, I am unsure of my age when this all began, but I was thirteen years old when it was finally reported.

It was the morning I was referring to above when I was getting ready for school. He did his usual sick and twisted thing, and then I got on the school bus. I was crying and emotionally exhausted because I had had enough of this abuse. For years it went on, and the only person I told was Ann, but it was not long after she knew before everyone else did too. She sat with me on the bus and tried to comfort me, but I think she was tired of seeing me upset, knowing what I was living in and not being able to help. She looked at me and said,

"Amanda, if you don't tell someone, I will." I believed her too. I got to school and was literally freaking out. I ended up having a panic attack in the cafeteria, and let me tell you, I thought I was dying.

I was so consumed by fear that I can't even remember how I got to the school nurse. The nurse told me what was going on, that she thought I was having a panic attack. I will never forget what she said next: "If you have something to say, you need to say it. Your nerves can and will kill you." I believed her too; I really thought I was dying. I was so afraid of my friend telling someone that I panicked and told someone myself—and an adult, at that. I was overwhelmed. What had I just done? Here was a new fear—a fear of him finding out I had opened my mouth.

I felt so many emotions as I wrote my statement on a piece of blank white computer paper. Anger, fear, sadness, relief—it was all too much, and now I was informed I had to tell my mom. I don't really know what I expected when I told my mom . . . maybe she would help me? What if she became mad at me? She said, "I hope you don't think this is funny, because it's not." Did she seriously not believe me? Oh, my goodness, who would think this was a joke? I wished it had been a cruel prank and that none of it ever happened, but that was not the case. She told me to go home, lock my bedroom door, and just tell him I had a headache until she could figure something out. I was so angry. How was that going to stop him from hurting me further? If anything, it made me even more vulnerable. Looking back at this now, I realize how much of a toll this must have taken on her and she needed to process, just as much as I did.

I never expressed my gratitude to Ann for giving me the opportunity to speak out all those years ago. Even though I was angry with her at the time, I think a part of me was relieved as well. Right before I told her of the abuse, my stepfather did something that left me shaking in fear. He made my brother and me watch a pornography video with him. I was mortified and disgusted at the images in front of my face. I was so afraid because this was the first inappropriate thing he had done with someone else in the room. I remember thinking the entire time, *Where is he going with this? Is he trying to involve my brother too?* Nothing ever came of that encounter, and I was beyond relieved. To this day, I believe that if the abuse had not been reported soon after that, he would have brought my brother into the bedroom to take part in our "playtime."

I went home the day the abuse was reported and stated I had a headache, as I had been instructed. Lucky for me, I guess he wasn't feeling up to his usual antics because he left me alone. Later when I returned to school, I received a visit from the Department of Human Services. I was called into a room to give my statement to a social worker or an investigator; I am not sure what she was, only that she was from DHS and was going to "help me." I put that in quotations because I did not receive much help from her. She lied to me; she told me, "We are going to investigate him. He will not know anything, and we are going to keep you safe." I felt safe when she told me that, but then a few days later, I got called to the office at school. I was told my parents were on their way to get me, and we were going to the DHS office. Panic almost became my new best friend because I lived in a constant state of it. I got in the car, and we headed to my certain doom, in silence.

When we arrived, we were called into separate rooms, and I had to answer more questions, as did my stepfather, mother, brother, and sisters. Then we went into a room together, and from the look on my stepdad's face, I could tell he knew what I had done. I remember perfectly the room we were in. There was someone behind a desk, and I was in front of them being interrogated like a criminal while my family, including my stepfather, sat to my right against the other wall, glaring at me. The person at the desk told me, "There is a place for people like you where you can go and talk about it." What? He hurt me! He was the bad guy, and *I* was being sent away? I had questioned *why* in my past when the abuse first started—why he had chosen to hurt me—but I never once blamed myself and never asked what I had done to entice him or deserve what he was doing to me . . . at least, not until now. Now I was questioning my own actions. Did I do something wrong?

What happened next was the biggest shock of all: they sent us home. I got in the car with my abuser and had to listen to how I had destroyed my family and how I was the biggest liar in the world. I *hated* this man. I hated the legal system that had obviously failed me. I hated everyone in the car, and every adult, especially the ones in my life who had let me down. Everyone became the enemy, and I was in this all alone, once again. As soon as we got home, I ran to my best friend's house, which turned out great because I ended up staying for a few days while he packed his stuff, moved out of our house, and said his good-byes. I ended up moving to Georgia to live with my biological father because of the investigation and the fact that I felt hated by every person in my family. I felt unwanted, like no one believed what I was saying was the truth. I was so let down.

———◦◦———

I began feeling hated even before the abuse was reported. I felt as if my siblings despised me. I got all of Daddy's free time. I got the unwanted playtime alone in his bedroom. They would be home sometimes while the abuse was taking place. They would bang on our parents' bedroom door, wanting to be involved in the seemingly innocent time that we were spending together. I had all of his attention, and they were jealous. They did not know, of course, what was really taking place behind the closed doors. I kept it that way and allowed them to hate me because I felt it kept them safe from the truth. For years after the abuse was reported, my sisters still had negative feelings towards me. They did not know the reason our parents had divorced was because their dad had sexually abused me. They blamed me for the divorce but did not know why I was to blame. I did not want them to know because I wanted to protect their innocence. I did not want them to see the world the way I did. My brother ended up finally telling the middle sister, and she in turn told our youngest sister.

The only good thing about telling someone of my abuse was that I was now away from him, but I had a bigger battle to fight: people did not want to listen. My voice was silent and insignificant.

Throughout all of this, even before the abuse was reported, I was not in church. I had gone to different churches here and there, but I never grasped the concept of having a Savior to give this brokenness of myself to. While I know now that God was walking beside me in those moments, I still felt alone because at that point in my life, I did not see the hand He was reaching out to me.

The only time I can recall ever crying out to God was when my mom had her car accident. This was before the abuse was reported. She was going to her friend's house, and I begged her to let me go because I knew what fate had in store for me as soon as she left. She would not let me go, no matter how hard I begged and pleaded. She was on her way home that night when the car spun out of control and hit a tree on the passenger side, destroying the car.

My mom was injured badly, and I remember being so upset for many different reasons. I was worried my mom was going to die and I would lose her forever. I was worried about her dying and us being left with this monster.

I was worried about what that meant for our future, and I was angry with God. I wanted to be in that car; I would have been in the passenger seat, and I would not have survived. I would have been delivered out of this hell that I was living in. It seemed so easy. I wanted to know why this had happened and why I was still here; it wasn't until many years later that I would get the answers to those exact questions.

After the abuse was reported, I went to a forensics interview and my mom divorced my stepdad, but that was the extent of it. He was never arrested. I fell through the cracks of the system.

He never touched me again, but I still had to face him on many other occasions, since he was still my sisters' dad. A lot of times, I would be blindsided by his presence. I would be somewhere, and he would just show up. Everyone else would know he was going to be there—everyone except for me. It was hidden from me on purpose, and I felt betrayed.

During the time of the forensics interview, I lived in Georgia with my biological father, stepmom, and stepsister. I didn't live with them very long because I just didn't know how to have a relationship with my father.

When they brought me home for the forensics interview, I ended up staying and moving back in with my mom. My mom and my soon-to-be stepdad had their first date the night I came home. She didn't want to go, but I told her she needed to. They have since married. He is an amazing man, and he is good to her. I felt bad for him at times, though. He was a single man with no kids of his own who married my mom and instantly gained four kids; two of them were so messed up from their previous stepfather that I felt he never stood a chance.

I was quite rebellious at this point. I had no respect for my mom or her new husband, and neither did my brother. We never wanted to be home or follow the rules. In my mind, my mom was still the enemy. I blamed her for something she never deserved to be blamed for. I was angry with my abuser and the system that had failed to protect me. I was livid with my mother and her brothers for continuing to have a relationship with this man who stole something so precious from me. How could they not see him for who he truly was? I realize now, of course, it was not right of me to think that way. I thank God for the way things worked out because it was just one more thing that made me stronger. I have always fought the idea that my abuse would somehow define who I am—like somehow by acknowledging that it could play a role in who I would become, it had some sort of power over me. The truth is the abuse did mold me into who I am today. While the abuse does not define me, it is a part of me, and it set off a flame that would spark a raging fire within me to fight for those who feel they do not have a voice.

For years after the abuse ended, I still struggled. I struggled with panic attacks and self-hatred. I was trying to find myself in everything that was wrong for me: boys, cigarettes, marijuana, alcohol. I continued to stay submissive in every relationship I was ever in, be it a romantic relationship or with friends. I never spoke up about how I felt. I silently struggled with these demons of my past.

When my mom remarried, we moved to a new school district. I had failed seventh grade at my previous school because of the abuse I was living in. I was skipping class and hiding in the bathroom all day because I was afraid to face people. I hated life itself and simply wanted to be left alone. When we started at the new school, they decided to place me in my correct grade versus holding me back again. I was overjoyed that I was not going to be held back again.

I made new friends—friends who would share their own testimonies with me about the abuse they encountered at the hands of their own monsters. It was not until this point that I realized this happened to other people.

Suddenly I was not so alone, and it hurt me deeply to know they had encountered something as gruesome as I had and sometimes even worse. I met Alice when I was in eighth grade. We quickly became friends and have remained best friends to this day. She is the only person who truly knows me—all my secrets, pain, and aspirations. To this day, she is the one person I can go to about something and never feel judged about the mistakes I have made—other than God, of course.

She was the very first person who told me her own testimony about being sexually abused. I have often wondered if this was the reason we connected so well, because no two people could have more contrasting personalities than she and I. This became a constant joke for everyone. Our teachers as well as our peers would say things like, "OMG, you two fight like an old married couple," or "You two are so funny—y'all are like night and day." They were right; we were like night and day, but that was the beauty of our friendship. She stood up for me when I would not.

Alice was a fighter by nature. I was dating a guy for a few years, and he was so wrong for me; however, I refused to see it. At my sixteenth birthday party, he and Alice got into a physical fight over a derogatory statement he made about her. I was mad at them both for causing a scene at my party, but at the same time, I was envious of her ability to stand up and fight for herself. I broke up with him shortly after that night because he and another friend of mine had made plans to "hook up" behind my back.

Soon after I turned sixteen, I got my first job at a local restaurant that served the best fried catfish around town. It was at this fish camp that I would meet my future husband. No one had ever left the impact on me emotionally that he did; he will say the same of me. The moment I met Ryan, we made awkward eye contact that neither of us could seem to break, but we never spoke a word. He later asked me out to see a movie with two of his friends, but even at this point, I did not realize he was interested in me. We went to the local theater as friends and played a round of arcade basketball. I obliterated Ryan's game by making nearly every shot and won the game. He looked wounded and I remember thinking, *Great job, Amanda—hurt his ego, why don't you?* His ego did not take as much of a hit as I thought because he kissed me that night. It was a bold move, but I could see then that he was not going to let me go without a fight. That remains true to this day.

I continued to struggle in my relationship with my mother throughout my courtship with Ryan, and my soon-to-be mother-in law could see the struggle I faced daily. She invited me to move in with them while I finished high school. Ryan chuckles about this moment because when she asked me to move in, it was a shock to everyone. She is a very modest, God-fearing woman, and for her to invite her son's girlfriend to live in her house seemed almost taboo. I eagerly accepted the invitation and moved in with my boyfriend's family at seventeen years old.

Before moving in with Ryan and his parents, my mother and stepfather were having some complications in their own relationship, and my mom moved out and to a new town. I was missing so much school at this point from having to drive from another town to get to school. Half the time, I would decide not to go to school altogether because I still battled some depression and had rebellious tendencies. I was going to fail my senior year of high school and not get to walk with my class-mates at graduation. My pride got the best of me, and I decided to drop out, get my GED, and just be done with school. I did so and got my GED a week later. Mind you, during my junior year, I was a straight-A student, I was junior class president, and I was in just about every club the school offered. My ego and pride got in the way, and dropping out became my biggest regret.

After years of dating, he proposed to me at nineteen in the same restaurant where we first met. Ryan's first attempt to propose failed. He planned to pop the question at a local Christmas lights display. The weather ruined his plans on Christmas Eve with a thunderstorm, so he improvised and brought me back to the first place we met. This is a memory I will cherish for the rest of my life because it was so perfect despite his original plan. I was engaged my senior year of high school, and while I admit that is a bit young, we both knew what we wanted and so did our parents. Alice once told me, "Imagine where you would be today if not for your mother-in- law." Truth be told, I cannot imagine where I would be. Ryan's mom helped me in ways that I cannot express. I aspire to be the type of mother and Christian that she is. I love her dearly and have never had so much respect for one person in my whole life.

My mother and stepfather eventually worked out the problems they were having, and I got married and had our first child. When my oldest son was born, it was love at first sight. I knew from the moment I even heard his first heartbeat that I would fight for him and always be an advocate for him, no matter what life handed us. He became my entire world, so much so, that when we found out we were going to have our second child, I spent the entire pregnancy in a depression because I didn't know how I was going to love someone as much as I did my first baby. I think that is every mother's fear, but as many of you already know, when I saw my second child for the first time, there was an instant bond. For me, becoming a mother brought on new fears: *What if someone hurts them? What if I fail them the way that I felt my family failed me? What if I completely fail at parenting and mess them up permanently?* I can assure you, despite those fears, my husband and I are raising two amazing little boys who are God-fearing and adored beyond words.

Just a few short years ago, my husband and I experienced a new challenge in life. While I was in nursing school, I lived in a constant state of stress. I began to experience panic attacks again and started blacking out in rooms full of people. I was instantly brought back to that same bedroom and experienced the same abuse all over again. My husband was acting out in anger, and I didn't feel like he was putting his family first a lot of times and began to associate him with my abuser. When my husband would get angry over something, I would cower in the same fear that I did as a child. This really took a toll on our marriage, and I decided to move out. It was not an easy decision to make, especially since I was in nursing school with no job and two small children; nevertheless, I moved into my mom's house with our two boys. My husband was hurt deeply, but he never stopped fighting to get us back home. He signed us up for marriage counseling, and I agreed to go; he also started anger management courses. The marriage counseling helped tremendously; the counselor made mention of me coming to sessions alone to discuss the abuse and felt I might have posttraumatic stress disorder, but I was not ready at that point and declined.

My husband grew up in church, and we attended the Apostolic church he was raised in. I have been going to this church since the beginning of our relationship. When Ryan first invited me to go to church with him, he was so nervous, and to be honest, so was I. I had never attended an Apostolic church before and did not know what to expect. When I went for the first time, I knew immediately this was where I needed to be. I had never felt such a presence of God before in my life, and there was no doubt in my mind that His Spirit was in that church. When I asked Ryan if I could come back the next Sunday, he was relieved and beyond excited. This became my home church. For the first time in my life, I began to see what I was missing.

One night we had an evangelist visit our church to give a message on forgiveness. I felt as if every word that rolled off her tongue was meant for me, and that God was urging me to let go. She asked everyone in the church to get a tissue, and whatever it was that we were holding onto spiritually, to place it in the tissue and simply let it go. It was that simple. Give it to God and do not pick it back up. I began my journey towards forgiveness for my abuser that night. Forgiving him was not an instant thing for me; it took time. It seemed as if God had to chip away all the anger and hatred one piece at a time. I was open to the idea of forgiveness for the first time in my life, and while that left a huge impact on my spirit, I struggled to keep pride out of the way.

December 11, 2013, 8:44 a.m.

I tell myself I'm over this
I tell myself I'm done

That I will overcome this
And that I've finally won

But in my dreams lies the truth
It's there I relive the hell you put me through

Your soul is dark
Black is your heart
I ask myself daily when does the healing start

Without a doubt you're the devil in disguise
You constantly haunt me with your nasty eyes

The day you're back in hell will not come soon
Then I pray my dreams will be made new

You tore me
You broke me

You stole something from me that I can
never have back
It's like a cloud that follows me—I've never experienced one so black

Will you ever stop
Haven't you hurt me enough

I see you every time I close my eyes
Can't you see you've already won

My fear makes me weak
My hate makes me wrong
Yet you stay in my head like a terrible song

I pray one day you'll know the pain I know—
The emotional, physical, and psychological

Stay out of my dreams
Stay out of my life

Let me enjoy who I am now, a mother and a wife

I wish your face never existed in my mind
Because I am done pretending to be kind

I wish the world knew—no, I wish it would believe me
But I guess that's the beauty of this for you at least

Knowing you'll never read this sickens me

I hate you—I will never wish you well
I simply wish you'd return to hell

CHAPTER SEVEN

AMANDA: JOURNEY TO HEALING

*And be kind, to one another, tenderhearted, forgiving
one another, even as God in Christ forgave you.*

Ephesians 4:32 NKJV

I struggled for many years. I was torn between
wanting to forgive him for what he had done and
still being hindered by the power he had over me. I had
the memories of those dark times, and so did he. The
only difference between our memories of the relationship
between us was that he got to still enjoy the thoughts
in his mind, while I was left to deal with the brokenness
he left me with. I struggled, while he relished in the joy
he got from his acts of terror. It did not seem fair to me

that I was still left with the pain and he still got the pleasure.

During our separation, my husband found refuge in the church and grew closer to God. He fought for his wife and kids to be in church and never stopped praying that we would come home. The day I decided to go home, we had an argument over something stupid that I made entirely more dramatic than it should have been because I was angry and prideful. I went back home to my mom's house and was sitting in the car, and suddenly it was as if I could hear God speak to me: *What are you doing? He is not the one you are angry with.*

I was the reason my marriage was falling apart, and in the process, my kids were being damaged from the separation. I was failing them. I called my husband and told him we were coming home, and he cried. I left all of our things at my mom's house and went home.

After the separation, my husband changed completely. He no longer acted out in anger; he was more understanding and open and put effort into putting us first. He has stated many times that he now has an appreciation for the house when it's a mess and the kids are loud because he knows what it's like to be empty and silent. We got back into church, and I started feeling God mold me into a new person. If you have ever felt a pull on your heart from God, you understand when I say it was very uncomfortable. I was having to deal with things I had fought so hard to ignore.

I continued in nursing school and finally graduated. I still battled panic attacks and debilitating blackouts, but I was also suppressing my emotions because I was fighting what happened and running from God. When I graduated from nursing school, it was my redemption from dropping out of high school. I was so proud to be a nurse because of the amount of compassion I had for people. It's always been ironic to me that I care for people as much as I do, because I've been hurt by every person I've ever come across. I know now that it was just another lesson to be learned from God.

I have always considered compassion to be both a blessing and a curse. Before I graduated from the nursing program, I had already accepted my first job as a nurse. While in clinical rotations at the local hospital, I met the town's neurologist, and he presented me with the opportunity to interview for a position as his nurse. Within two weeks of meeting him, I had interviewed for the position and accepted the job offer.

The clinic that I would be working for had never hired a nursing student, but they took a chance on me. I worked as a tech until I took and passed my state boards and received my nursing license. In fact, the day I received word I had passed and was now licensed, I was at work surrounded by my wonderful coworkers who had become more like a family. I celebrated at work but later went home to cry my eyes out because I was so afraid that I was going to accidentally injure someone and ruin my life forever. This is funny to me now, but it was a serious fear for some time after I became a nurse.

After working in the clinic for about six months, I kept feeling pulled to a greater purpose. I did not feel like I was making a difference for people the way I wanted to. One Sunday I sat down at my computer and saw two home health positions open at two different agencies. I knew this was impossible—I was a brand-new nurse with very little experience—but I heard God speak to me. He said, *Amanda, trust in Me. I will lead you where I want you to go.* With that I applied for both positions, and the next day at work, I gave my letter of resignation.

Over the next few days, both companies called to set up an interview, one on Wednesday and one on Friday. My manager at the clinic allowed me to interview on my lunch breaks. That Friday after I returned to work from my interview with one company, I got a text message from the manager at the other company with a job offer. I remember looking at my phone in disbelief. *Did I read this text correctly?* In a matter of two weeks, God provided me a way to shut the door on one part of my career and opened another. Let me say again, only God could have done this. I had very little experience and never considered home health to be an option for me because most home health agencies do not hire LPNs.

On my first day with this new company, I remember walking in and thinking, *What have I gotten myself into?* There was complete chaos unraveling all around me. There were boxes, parts of what used to be desks, office supplies, and people everywhere I turned. I soon found out that on my very first day of work, the company was moving to a new building, and it was all hands-on deck. Given my upbringing, I have always been an adaptive kind of person. I learned to adjust to whatever situation I was faced with, in hopes that soon it would become my new normal. This philosophy has been the foundation from which I have built my life, so it was no surprise when I jumped in and started packing boxes full of office supplies like it was the most normal thing to do.

While packing and moving, I was also introduced to the staff. Little did I know, these new faces and personalities would become more like family than coworkers. Among my new coworkers was a kind-spirited young woman name Dawn. There was something so familiar about this person in front of me, and in an instant, I knew why. This was not the first time I had met her.

I had met Dawn seventeen years prior at that backyard Bible club in the summer of 1999. Here she was,

Princess Dawn, a nurse at the same agency I'd just taken a job at—a job I thought I had no chance at landing—and in a completely different town—a town that neither of us was from. *How is this possible?* I wanted to say something then, but I knew the timing was not right. I knew where the conversation would lead for me but had no clue that she would relate. For months I wanted to ask her about that summer, but I never could find the right moment until one fateful Saturday morning. Dawn had invited me to her home for a business launch for a skin-care company she had recently become affiliated with.

The Friday night before I was to go to her home, God kept telling me I had to talk to her about that summer. It was all I could think about. God has a way of being heard when He has something to say; however, most of the time we don't listen until He is practically screaming at us—and believe me when I say God was screaming at me.

Saturday arrived, and I was beyond nervous because I was bringing my children along with me, and my youngest is a handful, to say the least. I had such a hard time focusing that morning on anything other than God. I kept hearing Him say, *Tell her, tell her.*

I arrived at Dawn's house without any knowledge of what God had been working on for the past seventeen-plus years. My little ones eagerly ran off to play with their new playmates (Dawn has two girls around the same ages of my boys), giving Dawn and me a moment to talk.

I started with, "Do you know where Glendale is?" She said she did, and I have since found out she thought I was going to ask her about a patient. I asked her if she had ever gone to church there. Then I asked if she had ever done a Bible school in Glendale, and she said that yes, she had done a Bible school there in the summer of 1999.

I knew it was she all along, but to hear her confirm it, I was blown away. I told her I was there that summer with my brother and sisters. The look on her face was priceless. She later brought out pictures from that summer, and the very first one she showed me was a picture of her with several kids, including my seven-year-old little brother with the biggest smile on his face. I was moved to tears.

I told her I knew this seemed crazy, but I had endured a very terrible childhood. I only had a few positive memories, and that summer was one of them. Dawn then started to tell me of her own childhood, and when the words *sexually abused* left her lips, I felt a sense of purpose wash over me. This was what God wanted; this is what I needed. I needed Dawn. I stopped her and was teary-eyed when I told her I had been sexually abused as well. From that moment, although I had forgiven my abuser some time ago, walls started to crumble. Someone had a very similar story, and she was sent to me at a time that I never imagined would impact me so much. Someone knew what I was feeling, and not just someone who sympathized with my story.

During the weeks to follow, we were on an emotional roller coaster. We were so blown away with all God had done. We were now inseparable and both felt the impact of what God had done and was continuing to do. We both knew this testimony had to be shared on a massive level and felt convicted to use our voices to raise awareness and advocate for the people who were left silenced by their abuse. Thus this book was born, and suddenly we had a purpose, a calling. No longer would we be silent about our abuse. God had redeemed us, and we needed to share that. We wanted to change the way the world views sexual abuse. We wanted to tell people to stop being silent about it, stop overlooking it, and quit being dismissive. We wanted to help others who were fighting their own battles. The decision to write a book was unanimous, and our journey was just beginning.

As stated previously, I have forgiven my abuser for what he did to me all those years ago; however, healing did not happen for me overnight. Many people mistake forgiveness with dismissal, as though somehow forgiving someone will dismiss what they did. That could not be further from the truth. I have not forgotten what he did to me. How could I?

Forgiveness is a choice. A lot of Christians see forgiveness as an obligation. In my opinion, it is more of a conviction that God places upon your heart at the exact moment He feels you need it most.

It was only a few short months ago that I again had a flashback and was brought back into that room. I was debilitated once again. I had also for many years experienced what people call "sleep paralysis," but I call it a spiritual attack. I would be in the bed and wake up completely lucid, but my body could not move, not even an inch. I would feel this invisible force pinning me to the bed. I could not speak or move, and in my mind, I would scream out, *Jesus!* I knew that if I could only say His name, this force would leave. I could feel that whatever was lying on top of me was pure evil. I would lie there in terror for what seemed like a lifetime, until suddenly I would jolt out of bed and scream Jesus' name at the top of my lungs. I considered this to be an evil attack simply because every time I experienced one of these attacks, they happened on days I felt empowered and had a mind-set to move forward from the abuse. The devil plays on our weaknesses. He wants us to feel powerless. He attacked me the best way he knew how to shake me to my very core—by pinning me to the bed.

I was also having serious problems with intimacy with my husband. I was struggling with our relationship in the bedroom because I was so afraid of his touch. This was so unfair to Ryan, and it was so unfair to me. The one thing that was meant to be an act between a husband and a wife, I could not do. I was livid; I felt as if my abuser had stolen my marriage too. I was tired of this and did not have enough strength to continue being bullied by the devil.

I went to church, and as the pastor was giving his sermon, I was so wrapped up in my prayer for God to remove this burden from me that I still cannot even tell you what my pastor was preaching on. This is important because I am a note-taker in church and incredibly obsessive-compulsive about noting each message. As I was sitting in church, I began to lose myself in prayer:

Father, I humbly come to You with a request. Please take this burden from me. I have forgiven him for what he did to me, but every time I am brought back into those memories, I am left broken and needing to find forgiveness all over again. If You don't take this from me, I will continue to break apart. I am self-harming by continuing this path, so You must take this from me—all of it—all the pain, anguish, and anger, even the anger I have against my family. I don't want this anymore. I cannot carry this anymore, not alone. I am not asking You to remove from my mind the abuse. I am simply pleading that You take away the emotional burden it carries. Help me, God. Help me mend my relationships. Open my eyes to the faults within myself, and help me to fix them and make the wrongs right. In Jesus' name, I pray. Amen.

Before I even knew what was happening, I had lost myself in praise, and I felt something hit me so hard it knocked the breath out of me. I literally was gasping for air; nothing had physically hit me, but spiritually God had knocked that evil burden right out of me. I realized God had answered my prayer and began to praise Him even more. Something that horrible had to be felt when leaving my body, especially given the length of time I had carried the burden. Since that night at church, the usual smells, thoughts, sounds, and bizarre things that would send me into a flashback no longer debilitate me. They seem more a passing thought, and I move on.

My relationship with my mom is much better since I forgave her and asked her for forgiveness. I apologized to her one night for something she never even knew she needed to forgive. I had asked her to meet me for dinner that night so that we could chat uninterrupted. By this time, she already knew what Dawn and I had been called to do with writing a book. I needed to speak to her about it, though. It was heavy on my heart.

We met for dinner one evening after she got off work. Before we even walked into the restaurant, we sat in the car and I started to apologize and ask for her forgiveness for the way I had treated her and put distance between us. I told her how I had felt, and that it was not okay for me to have put that blame on her. I didn't realize until then that she had blamed herself as well, but she had never brought it up or asked me about it because she didn't know if I wanted to talk about it. She wasn't sure if by doing so, she would just cause me more pain. She simply did not know how to bring it up, and neither did I.

CHAPTER EIGHT

AMANDA: THE VICTORY

You intended to harm me, but God intended it for good
to accomplish what is now being done, the saving of
many lives.
Genesis 50:20 NIV

*I*t is no secret that words hurt people, but they also
heal. There is power in speech. I have not been
able to speak to my abuser and tell him that I forgive
him. I honestly do not know if I will have the opportunity
or what I would even say. My forgiveness was for me; I
did not want to give this man one more second of power
over me. I forgave him because it gave me deliverance to
surrender to God's will for my life. At this point in life, I
pray he can find forgiveness within himself for what he
has done, and I pray he finds God.

It has been difficult to get to this point, to say the least, but with Christ, I get through one day at a time. My favorite scripture is Genesis 50:20 NIV: *You intended to harm me, but God intended it for good to accomplish what is now being done, the saving of many lives.* I now know what my purpose is.

I explained previously that I asked God why He had not allowed me to be in the car when my mom had her accident. I am given my answer daily: every morning when I wake up next to my husband, every night when I kiss my beautiful children and help them say their prayers, every day that I go to work in a career filled with compassionate acts for others, and every time I share this testimony or someone reaches out to me with their own.

I had a vision of myself carrying ugly, broken pieces of something in my hands. I was headed to an altar glowing with a divine light, and once I reached the altar, I instantly fell to my knees and presented this broken-ness to the light. A mighty hand reached down and covered the pieces, and when it was removed, I was staring at myself—only this woman was different. She was changed; she was every version of myself that I aspired to be. She walked in God's light and shared her love for Christ with every person she met. The brokenness that I laid at God's feet were the pieces of myself that needed mending. God made me whole again.

I want to leave you with one final thought: your life has been blessed. God created you and gave you a purpose. Sometimes we see that purpose at an early age, and sometimes He gives us a battle so that we grow into the victors we were meant to be. When he was on the cross, *you* were on His mind. Look at yourself in the mirror and see yourself through God's eyes. See your divine purpose. Rise from the destruction you thought you were meant to stay in. Release yourself from the bondage that has held you captive for so long. You may feel as though you were given a weak foundation in life—and so did I at one time—but then God blessed me with the tools I needed to strengthen that foundation. Remember this – you cannot choose your circumstances, but you can choose how you respond to them.

Lord, I pray that my testimony touches their hearts in some way. For those who know someone who has been abused—no matter what type of abuse that may be—I pray that they listen to them. At a young age, I found that every time I had to tell the details to another person, it was increasingly destructive; now I find it healing. I can finally speak about my past, and I will continue to do so without fear of the enemy, because You gave me that ability. God, I pray You continue to give others that ability as well. I am praying for a breakthrough in the fight against child abuse and sexual abuse. I pray that this reader finds his or her voice and uses it, or at least gives someone else the opportunity to use theirs. I ask, Lord, that You help guide us on this journey of advocacy and ministry. Lord, bless the person who reads this so that they may continue to fight with the proper weapons—godly weapons—and help them understand that anger is okay, but bitterness is not. In Jesus' name, I pray. Amen.

CHAPTER NINE

DAWN: THE TESTIMONY

*And we know that all things work together for good
to those who love God, to those who are the called
according to His purpose.*
Romans 8:28 NKJV

"God's timing" sounds like such a cliché phrase, but I began to understand this phrase on a much deeper level after meeting with Amanda that fateful Saturday. Things began to happen really quickly and fall into place in a way that could happen only with God's favor. With Amanda's permission, I shared what we had discovered with some of the other leaders from the backyard Bible club. We had all gone our separate ways in the past seventeen years, but I was still able to find many of them on social media. I felt it was necessary, as many times you never see a harvest, so I wanted to encourage them and let them know that they planted seeds in that community so many years ago.

Each person that I reached out to was blessed by what I told them. One young man, Joshua, was a freelance Christian writer and showed a deeper interest than the others. Joshua was a successful lawyer living in Washington, D.C., and asked if he could write about our story. Of course, we agreed.

Amanda and I were overwhelmed by what the Lord had done, and I was very thankful that she had spoken with the Spirit's leading, because I never would have known any of this otherwise. What she thought was ordinary became extraordinary, and God took what happened in the natural and moved supernaturally. Both of us were humbled but also had the overwhelming sense that if Joshua highlighted our story, we could be a light for others who had gone through similar experiences.

On Monday morning, I had a heavy prayer on my heart. I distinctly remember raising my hands in praise while I showered that morning, fervently praying for God's will. I then felt as if I needed to tell Amanda. It was honestly quite frightening, as Amanda and I had shared deep conversations over the course of the previous forty-eight hours, but in reality, we did not know each other that well. Nonetheless, I stepped out in faith, via text message. This was our conversation:

> "I prayed this morning for something kind of big and scary... I prayed that if there is a ministry in this, for God to open the doors for that to happen."

> "Dawn, I did the same. Last night we had an evangelist at our church and his message was 'You Ain't Seen Nothing Yet.' I got chills. God is working on something bigger than I could have ever imagined. I can feel it!"

This was just another confirmation in a series of confirmations. We had both, unbeknownst to the other, prayed the same exact prayer.

We mused a while over the wonder of how God had arranged everything over the course of seventeen years and were completely blown away by the door that He had opened two days earlier. We were also amazed at how we both had the same philosophy when it came to coincidence, and we both had a different variation of the same saying. Amanda's was "I don't believe in coincidence; I believe in divine intervention"; and mine was "I don't believe in coincidence; I believe in God."

Amanda then sent me another mind-blowing text:

> "Okay, this is going to sound crazy, but my
> aunt is a published author, and last month
> she started her own publishing company. I
> have been thinking about sending her my
> testimony to see what she thought."

God places desires on our hearts for a reason. If we are obedient to His will, He can turn those desires into things that glorify Him, but only in His timing. There was no way Amanda could have known that writing had been my only outlet for a very long time. I have always had the desire in my heart to write a book. I explained these things to her and told her that when I first met her, I was taking prerequisites at a local community college and was the editor of the literary magazine there, and I loved to write.

Thus, this book was born.

CHAPTER TEN

DAWN: NURSING
THE WOUNDS

Because you would forget your misery, And remember it
as waters that have passed away,

Job 11:16 NKJV

*R*eader, please understand that because I say that I write from a place of victory does not mean I am completely healed. At any point in time, I fall somewhere on the spectrum of brokenness. I need Jesus—every second, every minute, every hour of every day. If we believe Jesus is a quick fix to all of our problems and walk away with the fallacy that we no longer need Him in those areas, we will continue to miserably fail.

177

We often say "forgive and forget," but really, that isn't fair. We are not like God; only He is able to remove sin "as far as the east is from the west" (Psalms 103:12). If you read the opening scripture to this chapter, you see it says both "you will forget" and "you will remember." What a reflection of the juxtaposition in our own flesh! Our human nature is to hit replay on the video of our transgressors and dissect every moment in slow motion. We are weak; we tend to hold on to hurt and pain like it is our burden to carry alone. This is another reason we need Him.

Sometimes when you think you have accomplished healing from your experience, something unexpected happens. Something may remind you of someone you thought you had forgotten, when you least expect it. Maybe you awake from a bad dream and you allow it to ruin your day, or worse, you fall back into old habits. Maybe you get an unexpected card from someone you haven't forgiven.

Sexual abuse leaves many invisible wounds. Although this burden is carried by many people, the wounds are not always on the outside for all to see . . . until those wounds fester. Bear with me.

Abscesses develop when microorganisms get trapped in an area of the body where they are not supposed to be. Perhaps it is a bacterium that was introduced into the skin by a traumatic event, like a splinter. Maybe it is something left behind in surgery, like an overlooked sponge. Regardless of the etiology, left untreated, an abscess can turn into a more serious, systemic infection like sepsis, which can lead to organ failure, which can lead to death.

I never liked abscesses. As a nurse, I've seen many over the years. I have known many nurses who absolutely love assisting in the incision and drainage of such wounds, but this was lost on me. To me, these wounds were scary, unpredictable, and could be downright disgusting. Metaphorically speaking, the wounds of sexual abuse are the same. The wounds can fester and manifest themselves as anger, self-destructive behavior, or suicide attempts. Suppressing the wounds can lead to a string of bad decisions, diagnoses of mental disorders, and a general disregard for life.

But nursing those wounds? That leads to forgiveness and healing. I've told you my story; Amanda has told you hers. I know what it's like to feel as if you can't go on with life. I know what it's like to feel as though nothing will ever change. I know what it is like to be so desperate to get out of a situation that your hope of the future is the only thing you are holding on to.

I also know that allowing God to be sovereign in your situation means that you give up the reins of control and allow Him to reveal His plan to you. These things don't happen quickly, and as you have seen through our story, sometimes it takes years for God to fully reveal His plans; but trust me when I tell you, He has a plan for you too, His promises are true, and the Bible tells us that He can take any situation—anything at all—and use it for His glory. He works *all things* for good (see Romans 8:28).

Remember how I compared healing to an onion? There are so many layers to hurt, and we tend to cushion ourselves with the false comforts of righteousness. To heal, we have to get honest with ourselves and start peeling back the layers. Sometimes, as in my case, it's easier to forgive the person who assaulted you than it is the people who were supposed to come to your rescue (mother, father, siblings, other adults in your life). You may not be able to see it now, but those people who hurt you might have done things to protect you. I know that sounds crazy, right?

I have a friend who was born to parents who were both drug-addicted. Their addiction eventually led to this friend being abandoned by both parents, so other family members took her under their wing to help raise her. She had an uncle, a very godly man, and he took on the task of stepping up as a father figure in her life. As a teenager, she actually moved in with this uncle and aunt. She looked up to this man so much and was appreciative of the initiative he had taken to bring light into her life, but one day everything changed.

The uncle, without any explanation at all, uprooted her and took her to her grandparents' house. She understood that she would no longer be living at the aunt and uncle's house, but she did not have any answer as to why. She was angry and frustrated. For her entire life, she had been abandoned by the people who were supposed to be there for her.

She did not get her answer until many years later. Apparently, the uncle had discovered that his wife had a drug-dependency problem. He knew immediately that his niece did not need to be in this environment because of everything that she had already endured with her parents. He never slandered his wife, never revealed this secret. He was protecting my friend.

In the same sense, our heavenly Father does this for us all the time. Sometimes we ask why, but later we find ourselves shouting hallelujah over the things that He allowed to happen. The Bible is a roadmap to protect us from hurt, yet even when we sin or we are sinned against, He makes a way to heal and show His glory. Hallelujah!

Remember these things about healing:

- Sometimes healing comes through praise.
- Sometimes you have to look beyond your own perspective to forgive and to heal.
- Not everyone is going to be for you. Not everyone is going to support you or agree with you, and that is okay. Remember, you should only be worried about the audience of one—the One. Just pray for everybody else and love them anyway, even if you have to from a distance.
- We are commanded to forgive because we are forgiven.
- Blessings flow from forgiveness.
- God is faithful—always. He can deliver a message through you to help others.
- Sometimes you have to seek healing in obedience, even when it doesn't make sense.
- Be willing to step outside your comfort zone or what is considered socially normal.

I don't know if I would have ever told anyone about the abuse I suffered if I had not obeyed the Lord at nineteen years of age when He prompted me to tell my boyfriend. I was mortified with the thought at the time, but what healing that relationship brought to both of us! Imagine if Amanda had not ever mentioned the seemingly insignificant detail of the backyard Bible club from 1999, or if I had not had the courage to tell her about my experiences as a child. You would not be reading these words right now.

On July 3, 1776, John Adams wrote to his wife Abigail of what would come to be known as Independence Day: "It ought to be commemorated, as the Day of Deliverance, by solemn Acts of Devotion to God Almighty." (https:// founders.archives.gov/documents/Adams/04-02-02-0016) The last day of our writing this book ironically fell on Independence Day. Here we were, possibly doing the most cathartic thing we would ever do in our lifetime, freeing ourselves from a lifetime of experiences for the world to see, and our whole country was celebrating the date that we became a new nation.

As I wrote, the Lord prompted me to get down my father's funeral registry and look at it. It had been stored on a top shelf in our closet for a decade. I hadn't looked at this book in years and wasn't quite sure what I was looking for now. I opened the book, having forgotten that I had taken sermon notes from the service:

Now Absalom in his lifetime had taken and set up a pillar for himself, which is in the King's Valley. For he said, "I have no son to keep my name in remembrance." He called the pillar after his own name. And to this day it is called Absalom's Monument. 2 Samuel 18:18 NKJV

The preacher's message was that we all want to be remembered for something. My father would be remembered as a Merrill's Marauder, a quiet man, and for accepting Jesus Christ as his personal Lord and Savior. My notes included this statement: "What will you be remembered for?"

What will *you* be remembered for? The Lord can absolutely turn your pain into purpose. He can take that painful situation and turn it into something better— something much better than you could ever create yourself. You were not meant for mediocrity. Your life has a purpose. You were called to be greater than your childhood, your experiences, your career, your finances; these things do not define you. You were called for a greater purpose.

So . . . what *will* you be remembered for?

CHAPTER ELEVEN

DAWN AND AMANDA: JUMPING SHIP

$\mathcal{A}$t times, Amanda and I will receive messages either privately or via our Facebook page. One day we received a message from a woman who was inquiring about this very book. We explained how we were working towards submission of the manuscript and encouraged her to "like" our page and follow our progress there. The woman then expressed that she feared doing so, as someone might see that she was in agreement with what our mission was, but stated that she would share about our page privately to those that she knew were in the "abuse boat."

Abuse boat—that phrase hit us in the gut. We had discussed so many times that sharing our story with someone was like throwing a life raft to them to discuss their own problems, but the thing was, *we didn't feel like we were in the boat.* Amanda and I went back and forth about the "abuse boat" comment and agreed that metaphorically speaking, we had jumped ship and swum to paradise. Whereas many people were still on the boat, speaking only to others who were on the boat, we were wading in the water, calling out to them, "Get off the boat! The ship's going to go down! Jump!"

I mulled this over in my spirit and went to the Bible to find peace over this. I was led to Acts, chapter 27. In this chapter, Paul, a prisoner of the Roman army, was loaded onto a boat with hundreds of others to set sail from Adramyttium. They were led by Julius, an officer of the Roman army. Not long after they set sail, there was time lost, and the waters became difficult to navigate. Paul issued a warning in verse 10: "Sirs, I perceive that this voyage will be with hurt and much damage, not only of the lading and ship, but also of our lives."

That is the fate of the abuse boat. The voyage is hard. You lose precious time, wasted on worry, self-pity, depression, anger, fear, and self-harm. The waters become more treacherous the farther you travel, and with that impending doom comes disaster after disaster in your life, or loss of life itself.

Julius chose to listen to the pilot of the boat instead of to Paul. He trusted the pilot instead of the prisoner.

What he didn't realize was that the prisoner was freer than anyone else on the boat. Although he was shackled in the physical sense, he held the wisdom from above—wisdom that came from God alone. The ship became caught in a storm, and those on the ship began to throw the cargo and baggage off the side to even the weight of the boat.

How many times do those on the abuse boat take for granted the things around them that they need, disposing of them so carelessly? Sometimes their cargo comes in the form of the very ones who can help, but they distance themselves from what they need to sustain themselves in this life. Desperately, selfishly, they cast overboard the things that they need to sustain what they perceive as balance, but all the while, they're still on a ship that will surely sink. Healthy balance comes only from disposing of the emotional baggage that weighs you down.

They completely gave up on any hope that they would survive, but Paul had a vision. An angel of the Lord sent a message that God would deliver him, and not only that, but he promised that those on the ship would be saved as well. Paul proclaimed in verse 22, "And now I exhort you to be of good cheer: for there shall be no loss of any man's life among you, but of the ship." However, they did need to dock the ship. For two weeks, they sailed without any land in sight. Can you imagine how hopeless some of the men must have felt? Some of them must have thought Paul the prisoner was out of his mind, but then how many people held on to Paul's vision? How many wanted to know the same God that Paul knew? Paul's faith was steadfast; he had no doubt in what God had promised him. In verse 39, they thought they had found a safe place to dock the boat, and then in verse 40, they began to untie the ropes that held the rudders.

There is symbolism in this when you think about the abuse boat. The purpose of a rudder is to steer the boat. The ropes were holding the rudder in such a way that its path would be straight. The abuse boat heads in one direction and one direction only—towards death and destruction.

Before this recent study of Acts 27, Amanda had the following vision. These are her words:

February 19, 2017

I am sitting in church listening to the preacher's message titled "I Will Bless the Name of the Lord." He is preaching out of the book of Job. He says a single word that jumps out at me: *storm*. While I can still hear the voice of my pastor, I am now floating in the deep, dark ocean with waves crashing around me as the storm obliterates the remains of the ship I was just on. I am grasping for a piece of the broken ship and trying to keep my head above water. In the distance, I can see an island. I know in my spirit that this is paradise, and that the ship had no destination. For whatever reason, paradise could not be revealed while I was on the ship because no one was looking for land; everyone was lost. My eyes were somehow opened once I hit the water and began searching for dry land. I am suddenly appreciative of the storm. The storm gave me a chance to see my circumstances, and rather than being afraid, I have new hope. I love God, and He has blessed me with this metaphorical storm that I always knew as more of a burden. I release my grip on the board I am floating on, and as I do, the waves calm only in the small area around me. Light shines down on me. I lie back and feel the coolness of the water and praise God for His blessing. Just as I end my praise and start to swim toward paradise, I am brought back to reality, and church is over.

I realize why the light came to me only when I let go of the last piece of ship remaining. This piece that I expected to save me from drowning represents the fact that I have continued to hold onto my past even after God took it all from me. I picked up what I laid down at His feet. I could not see the blessing of the storm until I relinquished its control over me.

They began to run the ship inland, and the ship struck a reef and became stuck. The waves tossed the boat about in a way that it began to break into pieces. How many times does God allow our lives to reduce to brokenness before we are able to see His hand? The boat was broken; quick decisions had to be made. The Roman soldiers had actually planned to kill the prisoners to prevent them from escaping and swimming away; however, Julius wanted to spare Paul's life, so he ordered the soldiers not to carry out their plans. In verse 43, he commanded those who could swim to jump overboard and swim toward the shore. The ones who were unable to swim floated to shore on broken pieces of the boat. Everyone's life was spared that day.

Metaphorically speaking, there are some who are strong enough to jump off the abuse boat and swim to shore, but God created us all, strong swimmers and weaker ones alike. *But God . . .* He always makes a way. Some need the help of whatever they can grab hold of—a life raft, a broken piece of the boat, a piece of driftwood—to make it ashore. However, just floating on your salvation alone won't take you to the shore. You have to kick. You have to fight. You have to start moving, or you're just floating along, cast about with the waves in whichever direction the current wants to take you.

Reader, please understand our book is not a how-to or instruction manual (that would be the Bible) on how to overcome abuse. Each person's journey is uniquely different, but ours has been characterized by what we have experienced in our walk of faith in God. We recognize the comfort of being in the proverbial abuse boat. We were able to share our story with others in the same boat, but the Lord promised us more than that that. He promised us *life,* and life more abundantly (John 10:10).

We both lived on the abuse boat for a while, but frankly, the boat became overcrowded. We both could see what was in the distance: dry land that harbored a beautiful oasis. *Freedom.* Each day we neared the edge and studied the drop. There was fear that we faced in jumping overboard. We weren't sure what was in the water. We weren't sure if we could swim the distance. We weren't even sure if we would survive, but we knew we had to get off the boat.

We were so blessed to have found a friend in each other in our individual faith walks. One day we became brave, and we edged near the plank. We walked so carefully to begin with—holding each other's hand in the process—to help each other balance and provide support for the other. Then we decided we would no longer be held captive by fear, but would truly anchor ourselves in the Word of God. With this we found that we had power over our past in a way that we had never realized, and with that we discovered that we could walk on water.

#VOICEFORTHESILENCED

Voice for the Silenced, LLC

P. O. Box 409

Moselle, MS 39459

Email: nursingthewounds@gmail.com

Find us on Facebook @nursingthewounds

ABOUT THE AUTHORS

awn Compton is a wife, mother of two girls, entrepreneur, and author. She developed a love of writing in her youth as a means of escape, which served as an outlet of expression in coping with her abuse and also drew her closer to the Lord.

In 2016, she wrote a simple prayer in a Bible study for God to use her story to glorify Him. Later that year, she saw the fruit harvested from a backyard Bible club, seventeen years prior, in her newly formed friendship with

Amanda. *Nursing the Wounds* was born at an unexpected time; however, Dawn found that God had been authoring her story and intricately arranging the details all along to glorify Him in the most amazing way. Together with Amanda, they have founded Voice for the Silenced, LLC, to encourage others who have been abused to step out of their silence into victory.

Dawn has been a registered nurse for fifteen years and holds a master's degree in nursing. She is active in her church and community, serves as a Life Group leader and member of the praise team at her church, and attends ministry classes at a local church. She is currently authoring a second book with Amanda, and together they pray that their message of hope reaches many hurting souls for Christ.

*A*manda Schrader is first and foremost a daughter of Christ and enjoys sharing her love for God with everyone she encounters. Amanda is secondly a wife to her soul mate and a mother of her two greatest blessings. Amanda is a licensed practical nurse by trade and plans on furthering her education to facilitate her nursing career; she hopes to become a holistic nurse practitioner one day. While she has always had an appreciation for writing, she never set out to become a writer, but knew the moment when God called her to do so.

Since writing *Nursing the Wounds*, she has discovered a new passion for advocacy and ministry. Along with Dawn, she has shared her testimony on numerous occasions at different community speaking events and was featured in three episodes of the television show *Painful Issues Saving Special You* out of Memphis, which highlights testimonies of people who have overcome painful issues through Christ.

She and Dawn are also taking ministry classes and have cofounded Voice for the Silenced, LLC. Amanda has fallen in love with advocacy and feels as if advocating for people in a society that has silenced them is her greatest obligation. She goes through each day faithfully, knowing God will provide, and lives each moment with a fire in her heart to keep speaking up for the silenced. Amanda is currently writing her second book with her coauthor and friend Dawn, as well as a children's book for her eldest son, who has Tourette's syndrome.